3250
80E

Liberalism Reconsidered

Maryland Studies in Public Philosophy

Series Editor: The Director of
The Center for Philosophy and Public Policy
University of Maryland, College Park

Also in this series

Income Support
Conceptual and Policy Issues
Edited by Peter G. Brown, Conrad Johnson, and Paul Vernier

Boundaries
National Autonomy and Its Limits
Edited by Peter G. Brown and Henry Shue

The Border That Joins
Mexican Migrants and U. S. Responsibility
Edited by Peter G. Brown and Henry Shue

Energy and the Future
Edited by Douglas MacLean and Peter G. Brown

Conscripts and Volunteers
Military Requirements, Social Justice, and the All-Volunteer Force
Edited by Robert K. Fullinwider

The Good Lawyer
Lawyers' Roles and Lawyers' Ethics
Edited by David Luban

Liberalism Reconsidered

Edited by
Douglas MacLean
and
Claudia Mills

Rowman & Allanheld
PUBLISHERS

ROWMAN & ALLANHELD

Published in the United States of America in 1983
by Rowman & Allanheld
(A division of Littlefield, Adams & Company)
81 Adams Drive, Totowa, New Jersey 07512

Library of Congress Cataloging in Publication Data
Main entry under title:

Liberalism reconsidered.

(Maryland studies in public philosophy)
Includes index.
1. Liberalism—Addresses, essays, lectures.
I. MacLean, Douglas, 1947–   II. Mills, Claudia.
III. Series.
JC571.L538   1983   320.5'1   83-8623
ISBN 0-8476-7279-4

84 85/ 10 9 8 7 6 5 4 3 2

Printed in the United States of America

Contents

Preface

The Center for Philosophy and Public Policy was established in 1976 at the University of Maryland in College Park to conduct research into the values and concepts that underlie public policy. Most other research into public policy is empirical: it assesses costs, describes constituencies, and makes predictions. The Center's research is conceptual and normative. It investigates the structure of arguments and the nature of values relevant to the formation, justification, and criticism of public policy. The results of its research are disseminated through workshops, conferences, teaching materials, the Center's newsletter, and books like this one. The Center enjoys the general support of the Rockefeller Brothers Fund.

This is the sixth volume of the Maryland Studies in Public Philosophy. Previous volumes, listed across from the title page, dealt with the welfare system, the significance of national boundaries, immigration, energy policy, and military manpower policies. Forthcoming studies will look at issues concerning risk policy, air pollution, endangered species, and a number of other areas of public concern.

The chapters in this book grew out of papers presented at a conference on "Liberalism: Does It Mean Anything Today?" sponsored by the Center for Philosophy and Public Policy, which was held at the University of Maryland, April 1–3, 1982. Ronald Dworkin's essay, "Neutrality, Equality, and Liberty," appeared originally in *The New York Review of Books*, and we gratefully acknowledge their permission to reprint it here. The views expressed by the individual contributors to this volume are, of course, their own and not necessarily those of the Center, its sources of support, or the institutions and agencies for which the contributors work.

The successful completion of this book owes much to the unstinting efforts of Louise Collins, Carroll Linkins, Robin Sheets, and Lorrine Owen. Elizabeth Cahoon and Rachel Sailer are to be thanked for their expert work organizing and coordinating the conference to which this volume owes its existence.

DM
CM

Introduction

Whether we take liberalism to be a political ideology, a historical tradition, or a philosophical theory of the state, its meaning is today in dispute. The American political scene is marked by odd coalitions of Democrats who call themselves liberal and neoliberal, and Republicans who call themselves conservative and neoconservative, supporting a curious concatenation of policies. Some conservative Republicans advocate interventionist government support of the church and the family; other Republican neoconservatives abjure all but the most minimal governmental interference in the private affairs of citizens and corporations. Some liberal Democrats defend an untrammeled sphere of civil liberties; some of these same "liberals" defend a more active role for government in redistributing wealth and directing private economic investments. It is increasingly difficult to know who or what to count as liberal or conservative, partly because it is difficult to know what, if anything, those labels mean.

Likewise, liberalism is claimed to have diverse historical roots and sources of nourishment. Even within this volume, philosophers as different as Hobbes, Locke, and Kant are each proclaimed the father of liberalism. Liberalism is traced to the founding fathers' declaration of the rights that all individuals hold against any government. It is traced as well to the New Deal's agenda of robust government action to regulate the economy and redress economic and social inequities.

This is a book about philosophical liberalism, about the foundational principles upon which liberalism is grounded, as a philosophical theory and framework. While it sheds some light on present political debates, it is not primarily intended to give a theoretical underpinning to this country's major political parties or their platforms. Both parties make legitimate claims to represent (at least what they think is best about) the liberal tradition. Both appeal to recognizable liberal principles to justify very different courses for the nation to pursue.

Liberalism's starting point is the notion of equality, of equal respect for individuals as persons. This by itself, however, does not tell us very much about liberalism, for everything turns on what counts as equal respect. As stated, this central concept is neutral between liberalism and conservatism as political camps, for both profess a commitment to some notion of fundamental equality. It does, nonetheless, stamp liberalism as essentially *individualistic* in perspective—

those both far to the left and far to the right of liberalism will reject its emphasis on the individual as the unit of supreme value.

The notion of equal respect for persons leads in two different directions, which represent two strands of thought within the liberal tradition. One strand points to the individual's right to define and pursue (within limits) his own happiness, his own good, his own set of values. The cluster of concepts animating this strand of liberal thought includes liberty, neutrality, privacy—some protected sphere within which the individual can live his own life with minimal interference from the state. This strand of liberalism includes as well a (usually derivative) respect for the right of property. Some autonomous control over goods and resources is considered to be necessary for the individual's realistic pursuit of his own life plan. It favors a market economy, as both protecting property rights and allowing individual choices to determine resource shares.

The other strand of liberalism appeals to economic and social equality. It calls for positive government action to regulate the economy so that the market does not permit and perpetuate radically unequal life prospects for different segments of society. It is the bulwark of the welfare state: of federally supported education, food stamps, Medicaid, Medicare, subsidized housing, and Social Security.

One of the central questions taken up by the authors in this volume is if and how these two strands of liberalism can be made to fit together in a unified and coherent conception of the state. At least four different positions on this question are discussed: (1) that the two strands can be shown to be merely two sides of the same coin, one derived from the other; (2) that the two are not so tightly and logically related but are none the worse for that; (3) that the two strands taken together are incoherent, so that the welfare state must be curtailed by a primary concern for individual liberty, privacy, and property; and (4) that the two strands taken together are incoherent, so that a primary concern for individual liberty, privacy, and property must be replaced by a vision of society that is more egalitarian in substantive ways.

Ronald Dworkin begins his essay by identifying two aspects of liberalism that are "both under powerful attack." Liberals believe both (1) "that government must be neutral in matters of personal morality, that it must leave people free to live as they think best so long as they do not harm others," and (2) "that government has a responsibility to reduce economic inequality, both through its management of the economy and through welfare programs that redistribute wealth." Dworkin argues that these principles, far from being inconsistent, are both derived from a more basic and abstract egalitarian principle, viz., government "must impose no sacrifice or constraint on any citizen in virtue of an argument that the citizen could not accept without abandoning his sense of his equal worth." This principle grounds the neutrality principle because "no self–respecting person who believes that a particular way to live is most valuable for him can accept that this way of life is base or degrading." It grounds the principle of equal distribution by insisting that "no citizen [should have] less than an equal share of the community's resources just in order that others may have more of what he lacks."

This egalitarianism does not commit the liberal to pursuing "equality of result" in distribution, but only to an economic system in which distributive shares reflect the different choices to produce or consume that each individual makes in a market corrected for the effects of unequal (and unchosen) starting points. Dworkin thus defends a market system hedged about with redistributive welfare programs. He denies any conflict in theory between concern for individual autonomy and concern for individual welfare, however difficult in practice it may be to structure a political and economic system that is fair to both values.

Other philosophers agree with Dworkin that liberalism can coherently incorporate both governmental neutrality toward individual life plans and governmental sponsorship of redistributive economic programs. They suggest, however, that the connection between the two is not as tight as Dworkin supposes.

Michael Williams resolves tensions between a neutral government and the reformist programs it may sponsor (which he calls respectively "the Liberal order" and "liberal progressivism") within a view of the state (following Michael Oakeshott) as *societas*. A *societas* is an association of agents who recognize a system of rules governing how they may each individually pursue their privately chosen ends without agreeing upon any ends they will pursue in common. Rather than sharing goals, they share a notion of what rules should govern the pursuit of any goals. A *universitas*, in contrast, is a body of persons associated in pursuit of a definite common purpose. For Williams, the Liberal state is best understood in terms of *societas:* each citizen defines and pursues his own goals within a "code of civility." Liberal progressivism—the "willingness to see the government take on a larger role in securing the well–being of the governed"—is not incompatible with this ideal of "civil association" because Liberals recognize that civil association "will not, in modern times, be achievable or maintainable if no regard is paid to the economic and social condition of life." The Liberal can thus defend regulation of the market and aid to the indigent, though both are undertaken judiciously, with restrained governmental intervention in the private sphere. The program of liberal progressivism "is essentially defensive and compassionate, not the first step toward some utopian goal." For Williams, then, the two aspects of liberalism are related not conceptually but practically: social welfare programs are an instrumental means to realizing the ideal of civil association as well as an expression of the sort of compassionate concern for one's fellow human beings that has little to do with political theory.

Mark Sagoff joins Williams in arguing that liberalism's diverse policies and principles cohere more loosely than on Dworkin's account. Writing in reply to Dworkin, Sagoff denies that a coherent liberalism requires that particular liberal programs be derived from any over-arching liberal principles. In Sagoff's view, "There seems to be no necessary connection between the aspect of equality that is expressed in the neutrality of social institutions and the aspect of equality that may be reflected in [redistributive policies]." Sagoff worries that if the liberal tries to derive all the myriad programs liberals have historically put forth from any single principle of equality or neutrality he will resort to endless storytelling to exhibit the alleged egalitarianism or neutrality of programs that might better have been defended by a frank appeal to other shared values. In Sagoff's view, liberals like Dworkin are forced to defend environmental protection, for example, on implausible egalitarian grounds in order to maintain their fixation on norms of distribution. "[Liberal] programs," Sagoff writes, "might more easily and more accurately be explained in terms of a variety of values, including compassion, that lead liberals, in fact, to favor them. . . . they might better be justified . . . by . . . a sense of social solidarity, and a desire to relieve suffering." That liberal values form a somewhat ad hoc rather than principled collection is for Sagoff a strength rather than a weakness of liberalism: "The nerve of liberalism is to suspect absolutes and to reject them—even equality itself when it is presented as an absolute."

In a similar vein, Marshall Cohen groups together a broad range of "liberal" foreign policy positions without trying to derive them from any first principle less general and sweeping than: "political institutions and public arrangements should acknowledge and respect the moral equality of individuals." Liberal foreign policies—which include both (qualified) nonintervention in the affairs of other sovereign states and a call for a new international economic order in which the world's wealth is more equitably shared among nations—cohere together as expressions of liberal *attitudes* as much as implications of liberal *principles.* "Liberalism as we know it is more than a particular philosophy; it is a complex tradition of thought and the expression of a distinctive sensibility as well." This sensibility includes a tendency of liberals to emphasize "the potentialities of human reason and the common interests of men" and "a greater effort to see themselves as others see them."

In an essay examining the historical pedigree of liberalism, Nathan Tarcov attempts to show that the two strands of liberalism we are considering are at least loosely intertwined in the philosophy of Locke, perhaps the most influential of liberal writers. The two strands are often thought to have sprung from very different sources: Walter Berns traces the liberty/property/privacy strand to Locke and Hobbes; Theda Skocpol traces the welfare state to FDR and the New Deal. On Tarcov's interpretation, however, both strands are present in Locke, whether their relationship be tight or tenuous. He argues against the common view of Locke as a self–interested materialist, a thorough individualist whose concern with individual rights begins and ends with the right to property. Instead, Tarcov uncovers a Locke who, though beginning from an individualist standpoint, is committed to a rich view of sociality, and who appreciates a wide spectrum of human virtues that make for the possibility of genuine community. Thus, by implication, "a broader, deeper, loftier liberalism" encompassing both strands is possible.

Other authors find the two strands of liberalism to be in more fundamental conflict, however, and argue that a political philosophy that tries to incorporate both is doomed to incoherence. If the two strands cannot be made to fit together, of course, the choice remains which (if either) to affirm and which to reject.

Walter Berns, interpreting the views of the founding fathers, suggests that liberalism should be confined to the first strand: "liberalism is best characterized by liberty understood as privacy: the private economy, the private association, the private family, the private friendship, the private church or no–church, and all this with a view to a happiness privately defined." As in Williams's portrait of *societas*, government is not instituted to promote any final ends, but rather to establish conditions under which various diverse ends may be pursued. For Berns, however, this leads to taking property rights seriously enough that coercive redistributive programs lose their legitimacy.

Theda Skocpol and Christopher Lasch agree with Berns that liberalism cannot coherently found the modern welfare state on an appeal to individual interests in liberty, privacy, and property. They conclude, however, that individual interests are an inappropriate cornerstone of political theory, thus rejecting liberalism in favor of a deeper view of what it is to be a political community.

Skocpol analyzes New Deal liberalism as in several crucial respects a political failure. Primary among these is that liberalism failed to legitimate its new welfare programs in communal rather than individualist terms. According to Skocpol, the architects of the New Deal erred in seeking "to justify New Deal reforms as better means for achieving or safeguarding traditional American values of liberty and individualism." The New Deal's bold social programs required instead "explicit new definitions of state action as a desirable and enduringly necessary instrument of national public good. . . . People's inevitable dependence upon one another and upon a healthy public life should have been stressed to legitimize welfare efforts."

Lasch charges that "in theory, the liberal order should have collapsed a long time ago," victim of central and irresolvable conflicts between property and equality, and between individual liberty and social justice. Liberalism, on Lasch's view, tinkers with the worst social and economic injustices while leaving their underlying cause—the increasing concentration of corporate power—intact. As half-hearted reforms founder in economic hard times, they bring with them disturbing social and cultural consequences. Incoherent economic policies—mild redistribution within the framework of unchallenged corporate power—have had cultural ramifications that have cost liberalism the support of its traditional working class constituency: "economic and cultural issues are intertwined, now as in the past." Like Skocpol, Lasch would abandon liberalism's commitment to "the interests of the individual" for some form of social democracy.

In her essay, Amy Gutmann examines and partially resolves a different kind of tension engendered by liberalism. Liberals face a potential conflict between, on the one hand, the rights emerging out of *both* strands of liberalism (rights to liberty, property, privacy *and* rights to a decent social and economic minimum) and, on the other, the democratic system of government most liberals also espouse. "Liberalism," Gutmann notes, "constrains democratic authority. The results of democratic processes, like all others, may be tyrannical. Liberalism tries to protect individuals from democratic tyranny by granting them rights that can be used as moral trumps against the exercise of that authority." As the list of liberal rights grows—including rights to education, health care, and employment as well as rights to physical security—the scope of democratic authority is contracted: there are that many more limits placed on what the majority is permitted to rule. Thus many democrats resist the constitutional acknowledgment of liberal rights.

Gutmann reduces much of the conflict between democrats and liberal egalitarians by looking more closely at the sorts of constraints that even the most committed democrats are willing to impose on the democratic process. Two such constraints, which would authorize courts to override the will of democratic majorities, are the constraint of nondiscrimination ("The people must will generally") and the constraint of nonrepression, which requires "a free and fair process of representation over time." These two constraints taken together, Gutmann argues, may grant courts considerably broad powers to review legislation, both to eliminate arbitrary and irrelevant distinctions in the law and to ensure genuine political opportunity—which may well involve guaranteeing freedom of speech, free public education, and a decent minimum income. Thus, the tension between liberalism and democracy is alleviated. When the two remain in conflict, however, Gutmann would require that the value of democratic experience be weighed against the value of securing certain basic rights. In an indirect democracy characterized by vast inequalities of wealth and power, it is not clear that liberal rights would not weigh more heavily.

Gutmann, therefore, is willing to countenance judicial intervention in legislative decisionmaking in the name of egalitarian rights. Interestingly, Berns, who also defends the sanctity of rights against the possible tyranny of a democratic majority, opposes judicial activism; in his view, courts in recent years have not used their powers to defend existing constitutional rights, but to create new rights by counting as rights what Berns would count as mere interests.

On one conception, liberalism entails vigorous programs for relieving poverty and redressing inequalities. Whatever the theoretical merits of this conception, many people today (including many politicians) would claim that this ideal is no longer viable, that in a period of economic stagnation or contraction we can no longer afford the costs of such programs. Several authors in this volume address the question of whether liberalism's compromise between neutrality and liberty, on the one hand, and social justice, on the other, is strained in economic hard times.

Skocpol and Lasch agree that a decreasing economic pie calls liberal principles into question, making more plain liberalism's underlying inadequacies. Lasch writes that "economic expansion helped to smooth over the underlying conflicts of a liberal society," as prolonged periods of prosperity allowed the state to achieve modest redistribution without unduly threatening the interests of the better-off. As times worsen, however, liberalism's conflicts and inconsistencies receive harsher exposure. Skocpol agrees that liberalism's shortcomings "matter very much now that federal spending does not appear to guarantee a healthy economy and a steadily growing pie of revenues and opportunites from which every interest group can benefit with no hard public choices."

But Skocpol's reexamination of liberalism results in a call for an enlargement, not a retrenchment, of New Deal liberal programs: "reexamination should result in an *expansion* of community, regional, and national planning and in an explicit legitimation for a *broader,* rather than narrower, public sphere in U.S. capitalism and American society." With hard times comes an "opportunity . . . to set forth a vision of American democratic politics committed to . . . ensuring economic security and cultural opportunites for *all* Americans, in bad times as well as good." This for Skocpol implies moving beyond liberalism to social democracy.

Dworkin, however, denies that liberalism has nothing to offer as a philosophy for hard times. Even if he were to accept the doubtful premise that reducing economic equality through redistribution is bad for the economy, this would not justify imposing irreversible losses on a small minority now to stimulate economic growth for the benefit of others. And even if economic contraction is viewed as damaging the public environment in which all might take pride or endangering the prospects of future generations, it still would be inappropriate to call for a sacrifice from our society's most disadvantaged, unless it were clear that they, too, had reason to take pride in American society as *their* society and regard its future as their own. The present recession provides no reason not to treat individuals with equal respect and concern, by permitting them to define their own happiness and giving them a fair chance at finding it.

1

Neutrality, Equality, and Liberalism

RONALD DWORKIN

I

Liberalism has two aspects, and they are both under powerful attack.
Liberals believe, first, that government must be neutral in matters of
personal morality, that it must leave people free to live as they think
best so long as they do not harm others. But the Reverend Jerry
Falwell, and other politicians who claim to speak for some "moral
majority," want to enforce their own morality with the steel of the
criminal law. They know what kind of sex is bad, which books are
fit for public libraries, what place religion should have in education
and family life, when human life begins, that contraception is sin,
and that abortion is capital sin. They think the rest of us should be
forced to practice what they preach. The old issue of political theory—
whether the law should enforce a state morality—is once again an
important issue of practical politics.

The second side of liberalism is economic. Liberals insist that
government has a responsibility to reduce economic inequality, both
through its management of the economy and through welfare programs
that redistribute wealth to soften the impact of poverty. But the "New
Right" rejects the idea that these are responsibilities of government,
and Reagan's administration believes it has a mandate to curtail long-
standing liberal programs, like food stamps, Aid to Families with
Dependent Children, low-income housing, and legal services to the
poor.

What is the connection between these two aspects of liberalism—
its opposition to moralism in the social sphere and to inequality in
the economic sphere? That is hardly an academic question. Liberalism
has often been said to be incoherent as well as outmoded, just a

ragbag of positions developed by different politicians who chose to call themselves liberals. It plainly requires a fresh statement of its fundamental principles and consequent policies. How the two aspects of liberalism are related has become an important *substantive* question, because both the appeal and content of liberalism will depend upon the answer.

Philosophers have debated two competing pictures of the foundations of liberalism. The first—liberalism based on neutrality—supposes that the fundamental structuring principle of liberalism is that the government should be neutral in matters of personal morality, and that the liberal's concern for economic equality is simply the consequence of applying that foundational principle to economic discussions. On this account, liberals believe in equality because—and only to the extent that—neutrality requires it. The second picture—liberalism based on equality—is very different because it supposes that the liberal's emphasis on neutrality in personal morality is not the source but rather one consequence of a prior and more general commitment to equality, a commitment that already includes the ideal of economic equality. The social and economic programs of liberalism are therefore, on this second view, two sides of the same coin.

Liberalism based on neutrality has one immediate appeal: it does not take equality for granted, but rather proposes to show how some form of equality follows from neutrality. But this appeal carries a corresponding liability, because it makes liberalism much more vulnerable to the familiar charge that it rests on moral skepticism or nihilism. If liberals base their arguments on equality, then they can object, to moralists like Falwell, that enforcing any particular theory about how people should lead their lives—even the best theory—fails to treat people with equal respect and is wrong for that reason—even if such liberals insist that some kinds of lives are better than others. But liberalism conceived as a position of neutrality cannot rely on an egalitarian defense. It cannot appeal to equality as a reason why government should not prefer heterosexuality to homosexuality, for example, because it holds that treating people as equals is the result rather than the ground of moral neutrality. It must find some other answer to the moralists, and skepticism, which argues that beliefs about how people should live are merely "subjective" and have no objective validity, is an obvious and familiar candidate.[1] But skepticism seems exactly the wrong answer to make, because if the moral majority is wrong, and each person should be free to choose personal ideals for himself, then this is surely because the choice of one life over another is a matter of supreme importance, not because it is of no importance at all.

There are other, less apparent differences between the two accounts of liberalism. Liberalism as neutrality can, in fact, do only a poor job of justifying the kind of economic equality to which liberals have been drawn in recent decades. It can provide no effective answer to the most powerful arguments now made in favor of the Reagan administration's policy of curtailing or abandoning liberal programs of redistribution.[2] Liberalism conceived as a concern for equality has difficulties of its own, however. It assumes, rather than defends, a particular conception of equality, and it seems to provide no reason why liberals are not committed to much more by way of redistribution than they have supposed. It suggests that they are committed to some ideal of flat equality of wealth, which could be achieved only by such severe constraints on economic activity that individual liberty would be jeopardized. In this essay I try to show why, properly understood, liberalism as equality is not subject to these objections, and why it nevertheless offers a strong case against the economic programs of the New Right.

II

Liberalism based on equality supposes that the liberal's opposition to the moralism of the New Right is the consequence rather than the ground of his commitment to equality. This form of liberalism insists that government must treat people as equals in the following sense. It must impose no sacrifice or constraint on any citizen in virtue of an argument that the citizen could not accept without abandoning his sense of his equal worth. This abstract principle requires liberals to oppose the moralism of the New Right, because no self-respecting person who believes that a particular way to live is most valuable for him can accept that this way of life is base or degrading. No self-respecting atheist can agree that a community in which religion is mandatory is for that reason finer, and no one who is homosexual that the eradication of homosexuality makes the community purer.

So liberalism as based on equality justifies the traditional liberal principle that government should not enforce private morality of this sort. But it has, of course, an economic as well as a social dimension. It insists on an economic system in which no citizen has less than an equal share of the community's resources just in order that others may have more of what he lacks. I do not mean that liberalism insists on what is often called "equality of result," that is, that citizens must each have the same wealth at every moment of their lives. A government bent on the latter ideal must constantly redistribute wealth, eliminating whatever inequalities in wealth are produced by market transactions. But this would be to devote *unequal* resources to different lives. Suppose two people have very different bank accounts in the middle of their careers because one decided not to work, or not to work at the most lucrative job he could have found, while the other single-mindedly worked for gain. Or because one was willing to assume especially demanding or responsible work, for example, which the other declined. Or because one took larger risks that might have been disastrous but were in fact successful, while the other invested conservatively. The principle that people must be treated as equals provides no good reason for redistribution in these circumstances; on the contrary, it provides a good reason *against* it.

For treating people as equals requires that each be permitted to use, for the projects to which he devotes his life, no more than an equal share of the resources available for all, and we cannot compute how much any person has consumed, on balance, without taking into account the resources he has contributed as well as those he has taken from the economy. The choices people make about work and leisure and investment have an impact on the resources of the community as a whole, and this impact must be reflected in the calculation equality demands. If one person chooses work that contributes less to other people's lives than different work he might have chosen, then, although this might well have been the right choice for him, given his personal goals, he has nevertheless added less to the resources available for others, and this must be taken into account in the egalitarian calculation. If one person chooses to invest in a productive enterprise rather than spend his funds at once, and if his investment is successful because it increases the stock of goods or services other people actually want, without coercing anyone, his choice has added more to social resources than the choice of someone who did not invest, and this, too, must be reflected in any calculation of whether he has, on balance, taken more than his share.

This explains, I think, why liberals have in the past been drawn to the idea of a market as a method of allocating resources. An efficient market for investment, labor, and goods works as a kind of auction in which the cost to someone of what he consumes, by way of goods and leisure, and the value of what he adds, through his productive labor or decisions, is fixed by the amount his use of some resource costs others or his contributions benefit them, in each case measured by their willingness to pay for it. Indeed, if the world were very different from what it is, a liberal could accept the results of an efficient market as *defining* equal shares of community resources. If people start with equal amounts of wealth and have roughly equal levels of raw skill, then a market allocation would ensure that no one could properly complain that he had less than others, over his whole life. He could have had the same as they if he had made the decisions to consume, save, or work that they did.

But of course in the real world people do not start their lives on equal terms; some begin with marked advantages of family wealth or of formal and informal education. Others suffer because their race is despised. Luck plays a further and sometimes devastating part in deciding who gains or keeps jobs everyone wants. Quite apart from these plain inequities, people are not in fact equal in raw skill or intelligence or other native capacities; on the contrary, they differ greatly, through no choice of their own, in the various capacities that the market tends to reward. So some people who are perfectly willing, even anxious, to make exactly the choices about work and consumption and savings that other people make end up with fewer resources, and no plausible theory of equality can accept that as fair. This is the defect of the ideal fraudulently called "equality of opportunity": fraudulent because in a market economy people do not have equal opportunity who are less able to produce what others want.

So a liberal cannot, after all, accept the market results as defining equal shares. His theory of economic justice must be complex, because he accepts two principles which are difficult to hold in the administration of a dynamic economy. The first requires that people have, at any point in their lives, different amounts of wealth insofar as the genuine choices they have made have been more or less expensive or beneficial to the community, measured by what other people want for their lives. The market seems indispensable to this principle. The second requires that people not have different amounts of wealth just because they have different inherent capacities to produce what others want, or are differently favored by chance. This means that market allocations must be corrected in order to bring some people closer to the share of resources they would have had but for these various differences of initial advantage, luck, and inherent capacity.

Obviously any practical program claiming to respect both these principles will work imperfectly and will inevitably involve speculation, compromise, and drawing arbitrary lines in the face of ignorance. For it is impossible to discover, even in principle, exactly which aspects of any person's economic position flow from his choices and which from advantages or disadvantages that were not matters of choice; and even if we could make that discrimination for particular people, one by one, it would be impossible to develop a tax system for the nation as a whole that would leave the first in place and repair only the second. There is therefore no such thing as the perfectly just program of redistribution. We must be content to choose whatever programs we believe bring us closer to the complex and unattainable ideal of equality, all things considered, than the available alternatives, and be ready constantly to reexamine that conclusion when new evidence or new programs are proposed.[3]

Nevertheless, in spite of the complexity of that ideal, it may sometimes be apparent that a society falls far short of any plausible interpretation of its requirements. It is, I think, apparent that the United States falls far short now. A substantial minority of Americans are chronically unemployed or earn wages below any realistic "poverty line" or are handicapped in various ways or burdened with special needs; and most of these people would do the work necessary to earn a decent living if they had the opportunity and capacity. Equality of resources would require more rather than less redistribution than we now offer.

This does not mean, of course, that we should continue past liberal programs, however inefficient these have proved to be, or even that we should insist on "targeted" programs of the sort some liberals have favored, that is, programs that aim to provide a particular opportunity or resource, like education or medicine, to those who need it. Perhaps a more general form of transfer, like a negative income tax, would prove on balance more efficient and fairer, in spite of the difficulties in such schemes. And, of course, whatever devices are chosen for bringing distribution closer to equality of resources, some aid undoubtedly goes to those who have avoided rather than sought jobs. This is to be regretted, because it offends one of the two principles that together make up equality of resources. But we come closer to that ideal by tolerating this inequity than by denying aid to the far greater number who would work if they could. If equality of resources were our only goal, therefore, we could hardly justify the present retreat from redistributive welfare programs.

III

We must therefore consider a further and more difficult question. Must liberalism insist on equality of resources no matter what the cost to the national economy as a whole? It is far from obvious that treating people as equals forbids any deviation from equality of resources for any reason whatsoever. On the contrary, people with a lively sense of their own equal worth and pride in their convictions can nevertheless accept certain grounds for carrying special burdens for the sake of the community as a whole. In a defensive war, for example, we expect those who are capable of military service to assume a vastly greater share of danger than others. Nor is inequality permissible only in emergencies when the survival of the community is at stake. We might think it proper, for example, for the government to devote special resources to the training of exceptionally talented artists or musicians beyond what the market would pay for the services these artists produce, even though this reduces the share others have. We accept this not because we think that the life of an artist is inherently more valuable than other lives, but because a community with a lively cultural tradition provides an environment within which citizens may live more imaginatively and in which they might take pride. Liberalism need not be insensitive to these and similar virtues of community. The question becomes not whether any deviation is permitted, but what reasons for deviation are consistent with equal concern and respect.

That question is now pressing for this reason. Many economists believe that reducing economic inequality through redistribution is damaging to the general economy and, in the long run, self-defeating. Welfare programs, it is said, are inflationary, and the tax system necessary to support them depresses incentive and therefore production. The economy, it is claimed, can be restimulated only by reducing taxes and adopting other programs that will, in the short run, produce high unemployment and otherwise cause special damage to those already at the bottom of the economy. But this damage will be only temporary. For a more dynamic economy will produce prosperity, and this will in the end provide more jobs and more money for the handicapped and others truly needy.

Each of these propositions is doubtful, and they may well all be wrong. But suppose we were to accept them. Do they make a case for ignoring those in the economic cellar now? The argument would be unanswerable, of course, if *everyone* who lost because of stringent policies now would actually be better off in the long run. But though this is often suggested in careless supply-side rhetoric, it is absurd. People laid off for several years, with no effective retraining, are very unlikely to recoup their losses later, particularly if their psychological losses are counted. Children denied adequate nutrition or any effective chance of higher education will suffer permanent loss even if the economy follows the most optimistic path of recovery. Some of those who are denied jobs and welfare now, particularly the elderly, will in any case not live long enough to share in that recovery, however general it turns out to be.

So the currently popular argument that we must reduce benefits now in order to achieve general prosperity later is simply a piece of utilitarianism, which attempts to justify irreversible losses to a minority in order to achieve gains for the large majority. (The latest report of the president's Council of Economic Advisers is quite explicit in embracing that utilitarian claim: it argues that Reagan's economic policies are required in order to avoid treating the very poor, who will permanently lose, as a special interest!) This denies the principle fundamental to liberalism based on equality, the principle that people must be treated with equal concern. It asks some people to accept lives of great poverty and despair, with no prospect of a useful future, just in order that the great bulk of the community may have a more ample measure of what they are forever denied. Perhaps people can be forced into this position. But they cannot accept it consistently with a full recognition of their independence and their right to equal concern on the part of their government.

But suppose the case for the administration's policies is put differently, by calling attention to the distinct social dangers of continuing or expanding past programs of redistribution. We might imagine two arguments of this sort. The first calls attention to the damage inflation does, not simply to the spending power, savings, and prospects of the majority, as individuals, but also to the public environment in which all citizens must live and in which all might take either pride or shame. As society becomes poorer, because production fails and wealth decays, it loses a variety of features we cherish. Its culture fails, its order declines, its system of criminal and civil justice becomes less accurate and less fair; in these and other ways it steadily recedes from our conception of a good society. The decline cannot be arrested by further taxation to support these public goods, for that will only shrink production further and accelerate the decline. According to this argument, those who lose by programs designed to halt inflation and reinvigorate the economy are called upon to make a sacrifice, not simply in order to benefit others privately, but out of a sense of loyalty to the public institutions of their own society.

The second argument is different because it calls attention to the interests of future generations. It asks us to suppose that if we are zealous for equality now we will so depress the wealth of the community that future Americans will be even less well off than the very poor are now. Future Americans will have no more, perhaps, than the citizens of economically depressed third world countries in the present world. The second argument comes to this: the present poor are asked to sacrifice in favor of their fellow citizens now, in order to prevent a much greater injustice to many more citizens later.

Neither of these two arguments plainly violates the liberal's axiomatic principle of equal concern and respect. Each can be offered to people who take pride in their equal worth and in the value of their convictions. But only in certain circumstances. Both arguments, though in different ways, appeal to the idea that each citizen is a member of a community and that he can find in the fate of that community a reason for special burdens he can accept with honor rather than degradation. This is appropriate only when that community offers him, at a minimum, the opportunity to develop and lead a life he can regard as valuable both to himself and to it.

We must distinguish, that is, between passive and active membership in a community. Totalitarian regimes suppose that anyone who is present in their community, and so is amenable to its political force, is a member of the community from whom sacrifice might fairly be asked in the name of that community's greatness and future. Treating people as equals requires a more active conception of membership. If people are asked to sacrifice for their community, they must be offered some reason why the community that benefits from that sacrifice is their community; there must be some reason why, for example, the unemployed blacks of Detroit should take more interest in either the public virtue or the future generations of Michigan than they do in those of Mali.

We must ask in what circumstances someone with the proper sense of his own independence and equal worth can take pride in a community as being his community, and two conditions, at least, seem necessary to this. He can take pride in its present attractiveness— in the richness of its culture, the justice of its institutions, the imagination of its education—only if his life is one that in some way draws on and contributes to these public virtues. He can identify himself with the future of the community and accept present de-privation as sacrifice rather than tyranny only if he has some power to help determine the shape of that future, and only if the promised prosperity will provide at least equal benefit to the smaller, more immediate communities for which he feels special responsibilities, for example, his family, his descendants, and, if the society is one that has made this important to him, his race.

These seem minimal conditions, but they are nevertheless exigent. Together they impose serious restraints on any policy that denies any group of citizens, however small or politically negligible, the equal resources that equal concern would otherwise grant them. Of course no feasible program can provide every citizen with a life valuable in his own eyes. But these constraints set a limit to what a government that respects equality may deliberately choose when other choices are available. People must not be condemned, unless this is unavoidable, to lives in which they are effectively denied any active part in the political, economic, and cultural life of the community. So if economic policy contemplates an increase in unemployment, it must also contemplate generous public provision for retraining or public employment. The children of the poor must not be stinted of education or otherwise locked into positions at the bottom of society. Otherwise their parents' loyalty to them acts not as a bridge but a bar to any identification with the future these parents are meant to cherish.

If this is right, then it suggests an order of priorities which any retrenchment in welfare programs should follow. Programs like the food stamp program, Aid to Families with Dependent Children, and those using federal funds to make higher education available for the poor are the last programs that should be curtailed or (what amounts to the same thing) remitted to the states through some "new fed-eralism." If "targeted" programs like these are thought to be too expensive or too inefficient, then government must show how al-ternative plans or programs will restore the promise of participation in the future that these programs offered. In any case, cutbacks in the overall level of welfare provided to the poor should be accompanied by efforts to improve the social interaction and political participation of blacks and other minorities who suffer most, in order to assure them a more prominent role in the community for which they sacrifice. Reductions in welfare should not be joined to any general retreat from affirmative action and other civil rights programs, or to any effort to repeal or resist improvements in the Voting Rights Act. That is why the package of economic and social programs so far proposed or enacted by the present administration seems so mean-spirited and cynical. Taken together they would reduce rather than enlarge the political participation and social mobility of the class from which they demand the greatest sacrifice.

These observations offer, of course, only rough guidelines to the necessary conditions for asking people to sacrifice equal resources for the sake of their community. Different people will interpret these guidelines differently and disagree about when they have been violated. But they may nevertheless serve as the beginning of an overdue development of liberal theory. During the long period of liberal ascendancy, from the New Deal through the sixties, liberals felt confident that the immediate reduction of poverty was in every way good for the larger community. Social justice would, in Lyndon Johnson's phrase, make the society great. Liberals thus avoided the question of what liberalism requires when prosperity is threatened rather than enhanced by justice. They offered no coherent and feasible account of what might be called economic rights for hard times: the floor beneath which people cannot be allowed to drop for the greater good.

If liberals remember the counsel of equal concern, they will construct such a theory now, by pointing to the minimal grounds on which people with self-respect can be expected to regard a community as their community and to regard its future as in any sense their future. If government pushes people below the level at which they can help shape the community and draw value from it for their own lives, or if it holds out a bright future in which their own children are promised only second-class lives, then it forfeits the only premise on which its conduct might be justified.

We need not accept the gloomy predictions of the New Right economists that our future will be jeopardized if we try to provide everyone with the means to lead a life with choice and value, or if we continue to accept mobility as an absolute priority and try to provide appropriate higher education for everyone qualified. But if these gloomy predictions were sound, we should simply have to tailor our ambitions for the future accordingly. For society's obligation runs first to its living citizens. If our government can provide an attractive future only through present injustice—only by forcing some citizens to sacrifice in the name of a community from which they are in every sense excluded—then the rest of us should disown that future, however attractive, because we should not regard it as our future either.

Notes

1. Other arguments for neutrality, which do not rely on either equality or skepticism, have been proposed, but none seems sufficiently powerful. Mill suggested one: that society will discover the truth about the best way to live by allowing the maximum experimentation. But neutrality will, in fact, constrain as well as enhance experimentation, because some ways to live require an orthodoxy of morals supported by law and would be very difficult or impossible in a liberal society. See my recent article, "Do We Have a Right to Pornography?" *Oxford Journal of Legal Studies* 1, no. 20: 177. If experiment were our goal, we would do better to promote tolerance and neutrality in some communities, repression and orthodoxy in others. Some philosophers appeal to the idea of autonomy to justify neutrality. But this cannot advance the argument. Autonomy is a notoriously ambiguous idea; in its only pertinent form it is simply another name for neutrality—that is, for the idea that government should not seek to impose any way of life on individuals—and so cannot provide any argument for that idea.

2. I discuss liberty as based on the concept of neutrality in "What Liberalism Isn't," *The New York Review of Books* 29 (January 20, 1983).

3. In a recent article I tried to develop a theoretical standard for redistribution along the following lines. Suppose we imagine that people have an equal risk of losing whatever talents they have for producing wealth for themselves, and are offered insurance, on equal terms, against this risk. Given what we know about people's aversion to risk in the United States, we can sensibly speculate about the amount of insurance they would buy and the premium rate structure that would develop. We can justifiably model a system of tax and redistribution on this hypothetical insurance market, by taxing people up to the limit of the premiums they would have paid. This would provide more taxes and a greater fund for redistribution than we currently provide, but obviously not equality of result. See "What Is Equality? Part II," in *Philosophy & Public Affairs* (Fall 1981).

2

Liberalism and Law

MARK SAGOFF

In two essays, "Liberalism" and "Neutrality, Equality, and Liberalism," Ronald Dworkin distinguishes between the political program and the political theory of liberalism.[1] He argues that liberals in their political program favor policies that promote social equality, usually by making up for inequalities, for example, in access to resources, in opportunities, and in wealth. He argues that in their political theory, liberals require that the structure of social institutions be neutral on what he calls the question of the good life. The liberal state, in other words, leaves the question "what sort of life shall I lead?" ultimately to the individual to answer for him or herself.

I

I agree with Dworkin that a liberal state must be neutral on what may be called the question of the good life. The constitutive morality of liberalism—its requirement that people be treated with equal respect and concern—presupposes that many conflicting and even incommensurable conceptions of what is good in life may be fully compatible with free, autonomous, and rational action. A liberal state allows these conceptions to compete with and to accommodate each other within institutions or arrangements that are fair or neutral among them.

To clarify this point, let me emphasize that the liberal's conception of equality in the abstract functions at the level of *political theory* to prescribe neutrality in the basic structure of social institutions. At this level, however, the liberal's conception of equality does not fill in even the broad outline of a legislative program. It will only constrain this program (as Dworkin suggests) within a framework of rights.

Second, equality may function at the level of *public policy* as an ideal liberals bring to bear in the programs that they lobby for in the legislature. This conception of equality arises *within* not *about* political decisionmaking. Institutions that are neutral and fair and thus that conform with liberal political theory may produce policies that promote social equality, but then again, they may not. There seems to be no necessary connection, in other words, between the aspect of equality that is expressed in the neutrality of social institutions and the aspect of equality that may be reflected, for example, in policies liberals pursue, with or without success, in those institutions. A liberal state need not have a liberal government.

Dworkin suggests, however, that a strong connection exists between the conception of neutrality that occurs at the constitutive level of political theory and the conception of social or economic equality that is controlling at the level of policymaking. Dworkin describes these as "two sides of the same coin."[2] He argues that "the liberal's emphasis on neutrality is not the source but one aspect of a prior and more general commitment to equality in the abstract, a commitment that already includes the ideal of economic equality."[3] His thesis, then, appears to be that the liberal commitment to equality in the abstract includes, first, neutrality as the condition for social institutions and, second, economic equality as the goal of social policy. Once we understand what liberalism really is, in other words, once we grasp the fundamental principle underlying the political theory, we can fairly well deduce the nature of liberal social programs and policies as well.

If this is Dworkin's view, it is problematical because it is so symmetrical with the strategy adopted by Richard Posner and others whose commitment to equality in the abstract also leads them, as it leads Dworkin, to require neutrality in social and political institutions. This commitment prompts Posner, however, to propose "efficiency" or "wealth–maximization" rather than "economic equality" as a criterion for public choice. Once we accept Posner's political theory, i.e., once we agree with his conception of neutrality or fairness in the basic structure of institutions, we are also supposed to see that his social program follows, a program that consists primarily in the idea that a public intervention into private transactions is justified only if it can be construed as a rational attempt to correct a market failure. As far as I can see, this is Dworkin's thesis as well, except that he is concerned about correcting the inequities rather than the inefficiencies of markets.

The only practical difference between these two views may be that analysts with policies to defend will tell stories to show that these policies are required to make markets efficient (if they follow Posner) or equitable (if they follow Dworkin). At that point, equality arguments, like efficiency arguments, open a triumphal arch to the very cultural, moral, and aesthetic biases and beliefs to which the liberal's commitment to neutrality is supposed to close an iron door.

Consider, for example, environmental protection. Dworkin asks whether the government may acquire a beautiful mountainside as a park, thus preventing it from being strip mined for the coal it contains. A liberal, Dworkin writes, must find "a standard, egalitarian reason for supporting intervention." The liberal must argue that "government intervention is necessary to achieve a fair distribution of resources, on the ground that the market does not fairly reflect the preferences of those who want the park against those who want what the coal will produce."[4]

How do we know when markets fail to be fair? This is a complex problem. Coal companies and utilities have sponsored commercials to encourage the pursuit of "energy independence" through the mining of coal on public lands. Advertising agencies exist to create tastes for and social pressures to buy all kinds of products. What can it mean to say that markets fairly or unfairly reflect those preferences? Perhaps we should distinguish between a person's interests and passions; we should distinguish, perhaps, between the preferences that flow from a person's considered conception of the good life and those that are not so autonomous. How shall we draw this distinction? The way we draw it will determine, in part, the interventions that are justified on egalitarian grounds.

The problem is even more complicated. Suppose Mr. Liberal fears that markets, although egalitarian or fair, will turn every arcadia into an arcade and all of our natural beauty to commercial blight in order to service what seem to him to be frivolous and insatiable consumer demands. Suppose that Mr. Liberal believes that while an egalitarian society might allow suburban sprawl to conquer all, a decent self-respecting society would not. How can Mr. Liberal cope with these thoughts? How can he lobby for legislative goals, like environmental protection, that do not seem to be sponsored by his constitutive political morality but in fact appear inconsistent with it? The answer to this question, I am afraid, is all too easy. Mr. Liberal is likely to argue that policies that *seem* to serve elitist, paternalistic, or simply his own cultural preferences are *really* necessary to achieve a fair distribution of resources. Saying when markets are unfair and determining what policies are needed to "correct" them require the use of the faculty Kant aptly called the "productive imagination." Mr. Liberal may not have to look very hard for an egalitarian motive for whatever interventions he believes are right.

You might think that fairness is not the only or even the most likely reason a liberal would give for protecting the beauty and authenticity of the environment. The "equality" argument, however, appears to be the only one Dworkin allows. He would have the liberal, in this instance, contend that the process that replaces beautiful mountains with ugly mines will make a way of life that has been found satisfying in the past unavailable to future generations . . . so that the process is not neutral amongst competing ideas of the good life, but in fact destructive of the very possibility of some of these. In that case, the liberal has reasons for a program of conservation. . . .[5]

This example illustrates a tension in Dworkin's theory between neutrality and equality—the two sides of the same coin. How do we know what kind of opportunities future generations will want: those presented by a beautiful mountainside or those associated with the capital goods coal production could increase instead? To be fair to our children and our children's children, we must act on some conception of what they *should* want, namely, the beautiful mountainside rather than more commercial *schlock*. We cannot avoid paternalism with respect to future generations. The problem is quite general: while our preferences change our environment, so, too, our environment changes our preferences, which adapt to it. To what extent do policies that frustrate market outcomes provide a basis for future options and choices; to what extent do they encourage "adaptive" preferences instead? The neutrality of the liberal's approach to public policy may depend on an answer to that question.

Everything, or almost everything, moreover, has or may have a meaning; almost any environment or any product may be favored or protected for the sake of the way of life it symbolizes or for the values it may later reinspire. Consider, for example, the great gas-guzzling behemoth automobiles, the production of which, I believe, has been officially discouraged. Perhaps we should insist upon their production instead. After all, a life of profligacy, wastefulness, and conspicuous consumption that has been desired and found satisfying in the past may otherwise become unavailable to future generations and indeed to the future of those who now seem unaware of its appeal. Consider, moreover, the barge canals, railroads, and other forms of transportation that highway traffic has all but replaced. If we allow these to go the way of the two-cent letter, then a way of life may become unknown. Market processes would not be neutral among competing ideas of the good life, but would in fact be destructive of some of these. Shall we bring back the old whaling boats then? That was a romantic life. We have preserved the Staten Island Ferry; what about the pony express? What shall we save for our children, to give them options or opportunities to form values, and what shall we let fade into the past?

Liberals, to be sure, will insist upon a certain kind of neutrality in social policy as well as in social institutions. They take seriously the rights of individuals to make their own judgments and decisions regarding religion, sexual preference, lifestyle, and other matters of intimate conduct. When we depart from the question of the good life and consider the question of the good society, however, Dworkin himself concedes that we can no longer rely on a conception of neutrality, but we must look for other shared, public values.[6] It is not clear that liberals can derive these values from their commitment to equality in the abstract nor, indeed, that they need to do so. What sort of society—what kind of defense or environmental policy, for example—does the commitment to equality in the abstract call for and why?

Liberals, including Dworkin, sometimes write as if they have only one string to their bow, namely, a certain conception of economic equality (for example, equality in welfare or in access to resources). Liberals of this persuasion conceive of society and of all social relationships as Posner does, that is, on the model of a market. They may define the good society, then, in terms of an efficient market in which everyone starts with roughly equal amounts of wealth and raw skills. Since the world is not that way, liberals may construe social policy as intended to make up for bargaining inequalities (for example, by initiating programs that help the handicapped and redistribute wealth). These programs, however, might more easily and more accurately be explained in terms of a variety of values, including compassion, that lead liberals, in fact, to favor them. Why must liberal policies, even redistributive policies, be explained in terms of equality when they might better be justified instead by widely shared moral intuitions, a sense of social solidarity, and a desire to relieve suffering?

When a conception of social equality is made to do all the work of guiding public policy, it is bound to become as vague and indeterminate as the commitment to equality in the abstract from which, for some reason, it is supposed to be derived. The idea of social equality, in other words, is so fluid that it can be poured into virtually any policy container, just like its totally plastic competitor, the idea of economic efficiency. It is notorious that policy analysts who have command of the technical language can "justify" almost any policy in the name of efficiency by telling stories about what people would have done in markets but for, e.g., transaction costs. It seems to me that Dworkin invites precisely the same objection insofar as he opens the same opportunities to policymakers willing to speculate about what markets would have done but for, e.g., bargaining inequalities. This is the sort of story Dworkin himself tells in justifying regulations against stripmining to protect the moral opportunities of future generations.

I can see why liberals would want to derive from their political theory a single principled view about the structure of social institutions. This structure, after all, is the subject matter of political theory. Public policy, however, is not the subject matter of political theory, and thus liberals need not look for some abstract principle from which to derive the various values they support in the legislature, especially when these values may be defended better in more ad hoc and less speculative ways. Whether "equality" or "efficiency" is taken to be the touchstone of liberal social policy, moreover, does not matter, for both do the same trick; they conceal the substantive values and moral intuitions that liberals might otherwise admit to and thus they give liberalism a specious air of "scientific" neutrality. And so liberal policy analysts may treat us, either way, to speculation about shadow prices and transaction costs until Congress, mercifully, cuts off the funding and gets on with its less sophisticated business of political bloodletting. There must be more breathing room than Posner or Dworkin gives us between the political theory and the legislative program. Mr. Liberal does not have to tell the story about fairness in order to preserve the wilderness. He need not defend the furbish lousewort on egalitarian grounds.

II

In a discussion of equality, Dworkin divides preferences into three kinds. There are, first, *political* preferences, by which he means "preferences about how the goods, resources and opportunities of the community should be distributed to others."

> Second, people have what I shall call *impersonal preferences*, which are preferences about things other than their own or other people's lives or situations. Some people care very much about the advance of scientific knowledge, for example, even though it will not be they (or any person they know) who will make the advance, while others care deeply about the conservation of certain kinds of beauty they will never see.[7]

Third, people have what Dworkin calls personal preferences, by which he means "their preferences about their own experience or situation."[8]

Liberals may build their political preferences into the structure of institutions (by giving each person one vote, for example); they may also pursue them through policy decisions (for example, by making taxes more progressive). Some liberals suggest, however, that the only values they may pursue politically as liberals are preferences about the way that goods and services are distributed. (Dworkin supports this view by describing distributional norms as political preferences.) They believe the government acts primarily as a prophylactic upon markets; it intervenes only to make them more fair and more efficient. Liberals of this persuasion rule out impersonal preferences—respect for science, veneration for the arts, concern with our natural heritage—as grounds for public decisionmaking. They believe that these values express particular views concerning the good life (a preference, as it were, for certain kinds of preferences) and fear that policies based upon them will not treat everyone's actual personal preferences with equal respect and concern.

To get a handle on this conception of liberalism—to see what is wrong with it—let us consider Jones, an environmentalist, who cares very much that the wilderness be preserved even though he may never visit it. How should Mr. Liberal deal with this impersonal or public value? The liberal, as Brian Barry suggests, may analyze "Jones believes the wilderness ought to be preserved" as "Jones wants people to enjoy the wilderness." The liberal, then, may regard Jones's moral and aesthetic beliefs and the reasons for them as his personal crochets about what other people should want or enjoy.

"What underlies this view," Barry points out, "is a rejection of any suggestion that an ideal-regarding judgment should be treated as anything but a peculiar kind of want."[9] Liberals who take this view may, indeed, treat ideal-regarding judgments as "external" or as "meddling" preferences and exclude them from political consideration. To include them, as Dworkin suggests, would be unfair since it would count the preferences of wilderness-users twice, once to please them and a second time to please Jones.[10] The policymaker may also construe Jones's judgment as expressing a "moralistic" or "intangible" value, a kind of weird externality that markets unfortunately fail to price.

Why should liberals go to such lengths to discount moral and aesthetic judgments, in short, public values, when one might think these belonged at the heart of political discussion? An answer may be found in the liberal contractarian tradition, which provides a logical and historical basis for the view that the government should ignore or somehow discount the other-regarding or impersonal preferences of the citizenry. According to the contractarian tradition, people do not associate politically to debate, construct, and act upon conceptions of the good society; they form governments to protect and to promote the personal interests they already have. Locke, for example, argues that since the power of the state exists to serve the pre-political and personal interests of its citizens, it should be used only to police individuals, not to make them better than they are. Other-regarding and ideal-regarding judgments or preferences, then, seem to be illegitimate and impertinent intrusions when they become the business of government.

The objections to this argument are many, but two seem most relevant. First, no one has shown that rational individuals, forming a government in a situation that is fair between them, would choose to deny that government the power to promote impersonal or ideal-regarding aspirations providing that those aspirations are chosen through the legitimate political process. Individuals will insist, of course, on having civil rights to protect them from the power that political rights create. The rights that are intended to restrict the power of government to formulate and to pursue public values, however, may also function to make that power legitimate.

Second, contractarian theories tend to assume that powers not exercised by the government will spread evenly among individuals in civil society. Nothing could be farther from the truth. Civil society is hardly a Brownian motion of autonomous and atomic individuals cowering before the Leviathan. It is itself a collection of centers of authority and coercion, many of which may make the push-me-pull-you bureaucracies of government seem tame and unthreatening by comparison.

If the government does not give us a wilderness policy or an endangered species policy responsive to our impersonal judgments then the corporations will surely give us one based on some adman's conception of our personal wants instead. Which policy better reflects the will of autonomous individuals? May the government outlaw the taking of whales on aesthetic and moral (that is, impersonal) grounds? Would a liberal object to such a political action? I think not. Many liberals do support the protection of whales and this has nothing to do with satisfying consumer preferences, e.g., by maximizing the sustained yield of blubber.

I believe that liberals qua liberals may promote impersonal as well as political preferences by political means; they may strive politically, for example, to protect the natural environment, advance the sciences, and support the arts. These goals and the idea of the good society they reflect need not be derived from a commitment to equality in the abstract, although they will not depart radically from that commitment. Liberals will also act on a sense of human sympathy or moral compassion whether that intuition follows after their abstract political ideal or not. Thus, liberals will regulate the safety of consumer products, the workplace, and the environment to prevent needless suffering and not necessarily to give people equal access to wealth. Liberalism is not a ragbag of principles and beliefs nor is it a single principle or belief. It consists in a collection of intuitions and ideals that fit together more tightly at the level of political theory than in a history of humane and progressive legislation.

To see that liberals may promote impersonal as well as personal and political preferences, we may ask why preferences should be satisfied at all. No one has shown that the satisfaction of preferences, after basic needs are met, increases happiness; it may as well lead to disillusion and frustration. One's basic needs, to be sure, ought to be satisfied, but this is because they are basic needs and not necessarily because they are preferences. Why should it count in favor of political decisions, then, that they satisfy personal preferences or give people more of whatever they happen to want?

Someone might argue that preferences ought to be satisfied because this makes people "better off." When we ask what "better off" means, however, we discover that it means having more preferences satisfied, and so economists who make this argument reason in a very small circle. Someone may say that preferences ought to be satisfied because this is what people who have those preferences want. This answer, besides suggesting an infinite regress, seems to be false. Today, a person may want a particular preference to be satisfied; tomorrow he may be glad that it was not satisfied or he may regret that it was. People want their preferences to be satisfied at the moment they have them but they may feel quite differently about those preferences at some other time. Disillusion, experience, and enlightenment lead us to change our minds about the value of any particular preference we may have had. Thus, whether a person wants one of his preferences satisfied depends on what he knows and when he is asked. Every parent bathing a screaming baby must be swept at some time with an urge to drown the infant in the bathwater. Yet no one—certainly not the parent—would want this preference, however intense at the time, satisfied.

We may agree with Dworkin that a person's considered conception of the good life and the values that enter that life make a legitimate claim on societal concern and respect. This is what cannot be said of the passing or ephemeral preferences a person entertains, especially those that are created by the processes of distribution that exist to satisfy them. I cannot discover, then, a good answer to the question why it should count in favor of political decisions that they maximize the extent to which people have what they happen to want. I do not deny that preferences are often important to the people who have them; it is a virtue of a political system that it allows individuals freely to try to satisfy their desires as long as they do not unfairly harm others. Personal preferences, however, are not the only values that people find important. People may regard their impersonal or community-regarding preferences also as important; they may cherish their participation in societal efforts to achieve a kind of public happiness as much as they cherish their right to seek, in their own way, a private happiness. The individual may set as much store by his conception of the good society as he does by his conception of the good life.

In my view, a public policy is justified by the impersonal reasons that support it rather than the personal preferences it satisfies except insofar as these preferences may count as reasons. If personal preferences, wants, and tastes are the only or the principal reasons for or against a particular decision, then this choice is properly left to markets, which would rank the relevant wants on the basis of the cost of satisfying them. When the reasons for a policy are of a kind that need to be understood and criticized rather than priced, however, the ideal of the market is no longer relevant. We go beyond distributional norms or what Dworkin calls "political" preferences. To take people and their rights seriously government must respond to their beliefs, arguments, and opinions about the good society and not merely attend neutrally to their conceptions of the good life. I emphasize this point because someone might think it is the reasons that justify a policy rather than the people who want it that count in my view. I have not argued that reasons are more important than persons; I have argued that they are important *to* persons and in political decisions often more important than wants.

We may ask, in this light, what it is to treat people with respect and concern. To treat a person with respect and concern, I should say, is at least to treat him or her *as a person* and thus as capable of making or supporting policy choices on the basis of good reasons and not merely arbitrary wants. Insofar as an individual grounds his choices on reasons, however, he does not *choose* these reasons; rather, he recognizes or thinks he recognizes their validity—not their validity *for him* (whatever that could mean) but their validity for all members of the community or their validity *simpliciter.* These reasons, then, demand to be recognized, considered, and understood by others, particularly by those who in making public policy are supposed to be responsive to them. To treat persons with equal respect and concern is at least to consider fairly the reasons they give for or against a public decision and to offer them reasons in return. It is ultimately to let individuals themselves be the judges of those reasons. This is in the nature of a representative democracy; it is not in the nature of a market.

III

Socialists, conservatives, and liberals differ in the ways they deal with one problem I have touched upon in this essay, namely, the fact that our personal preferences may not be autonomous but may arise from social pressure, advertising, or some other kind of seduction, rather than from an examination of competing conceptions of the good life and the values that enter that life. The socialist believes that the reason people may be deceived, the reason their interests are less wise, noble, or virtuous than they might be, is that they have been corrupted by a bourgeois or capitalist ideology from which they must be liberated, by government action if necessary, so that they may share in the ideology they would have accepted were they not so corrupted. Conservatives locate the source of human weakness in original sin or in the nature of the beast; they conclude that radical or socialist cures are likely to be worse than the disease. The conservative believes that the traditional values and institutions of his society should be maintained, as Dworkin writes, because they "are better guides to sound virtue than any nonhistorical and therefore abstract deduction of virtue from first principles could provide."[11]

The liberal likewise may distinguish between persons and their preferences and thus he or she may recognize that personal preferences are not always autonomous and thus cannot always claim societal concern and respect. The liberal will acknowledge, moreover, that the individual may advocate through the political process certain impersonal preferences (for example, about the arts or the environment) that are more in touch with his or her conception of the good life than are many of his or her personal wants. The liberal, like the conservative and the socialist, then, may allow legislatures to affirm impersonal values, that is, public conceptions of virtue, although he or she will hedge this power (as Dworkin argues) with a doctrine of civil and political rights.

How, then, does the liberal differ from the socialist and the conservative? The essential difference is this. Socialists and conservatives have well-worked-out dialectical and historical arguments—full theories or explanations, as it were—of public virtue and of the good society. The liberal, on the contrary, has no such worked-out theory but proceeds by a *via negativa* to describe what a good society does *not* do. A good society does not wage an unjust war, for example; it does not permit its citizens to fall below a certain level of welfare; it does not tolerate racism; it does not let criminal suspects go without counsel. A good society refuses to trade a wilderness heritage for a bowl of consumer porridge. The liberal does not and need not refer to a single principle or reason for setting these negative conditions. They follow, rather, from a variety of reasons, among them, human sympathy, aesthetic judgment, and common sense.

Liberals advocate child labor laws, minimum wage and maximum hour rules, minimum standards for workplace safety and environmental quality, implied warranties, and compulsory terms in contracts, to keep people from ruining themselves and each other, even if this is what they would do in equitable markets if they were free to choose. These policies suggest an egalitarian motive, and no doubt there is one, but they also suggest a broad humanitarian instinct not wedded to any particular theory or principle. Liberals try to cut the losses of individuals and society while maintaining a commitment to pluralism. This is the way liberals manage human frailty or, if you prefer, the process by which free and equal persons attempt to live their own lives.

This leads us to the question, of course, how the liberal knows the interventions he favors (his "impersonal" preferences) are benign rather than intrusive, socially uniting rather than divisive. The answer is that the liberal *acknowledges that he does not know* and for that reason remains suspicious and critical of what he does. The liberal maintains his commitment to neutrality by having no single principle by which he separates correct and incorrect interventions; rather, in taking rights seriously, he acknowledges his uncertainty by setting limits to those interventions. A doctrine of rights, by restricting the role of government in interfering with the lives of individuals, also makes that role legitimate. The liberal limits governmental power further, however, to actions that appeal to the good sense and judgment of those whom they affect and not to an abstract principle instead.

Liberals may make mistakes—they may impose on people in ways that are subtly sexist or racist—and for this reason they are never above suspicion and never cease to suspect themselves. They attempt, therefore, to mobilize and to win the approval of the constituencies whom they affect. If resentment is strong (if bikers refuse to wear helmets, for example, or consumers demand saccharine) the liberal will back off and thus will allow the individual, ultimately, to be the judge of public policies and the reasons for those policies. This kind of respect and concern regards the individual as a judge of reasons and not merely as a haver of preferences.

I believe that Dworkin is correct when he says that liberalism requires the government to be neutral on the question of the good life. I do not take this to mean, however, that liberals must refrain from legislating their impersonal preferences concerning health, safety, defense, foreign policy, and advancement of science, and so on; indeed, much of our progressive policymaking in the last thirty years represents what Dworkin calls the impersonal as distinct from the political or personal preferences of liberal courts and legislatures. Liberals are committed to human equality, to be sure, but this commitment, too, reflects compassion and sympathy for human beings as much as it derives from a constitutive political morality. I imagine that if liberals could find a theoretical criterion or principle for distinguishing justified from nonjustified interventions—if they could derive policy from theory—they would no longer be liberals. The nerve of liberalism is to suspect absolutes and to reject them—even equality itself when it is presented as an absolute.

Notes

1. Ronald Dworkin, "Liberalism," in *Public and Private Morality,* edited by Stuart Hampshire (Cambridge: Cambridge University Press, 1978); Dworkin, "Neutrality, Equality, and Liberalism," this volume.

2. Dworkin, "Liberalism," p. 141.

3. Ibid.

4. Ibid.

5. Ibid., pp. 141–42.

6. Dworkin, "Neutrality," pp. 6–7, this volume.

7, Dworkin, "Equality of Welfare," *Philosophy & Public Affairs* 10, no. 3 (Summer 1982): 192. Italics supplied.

3

How Liberal Is Democracy?

AMY GUTMANN

It is a commonplace that liberalism constrains democratic authority. The results of democratic processes, like all others, may be tyrannical. Liberalism tries to protect individuals from democratic tyranny by granting them rights that can be used as moral trumps against the exercise of that authority.[1] Some rights have nearly unanimous endorsement among liberals: freedom of speech and religion, the right to be secure in one's personal possessions, the right against self-incrimination and double jeopardy. Other liberal rights are more controversial in part because they are rights of recipience rather than noninterference and therefore contingent upon a level of affluence that only relatively few societies have achieved. But these welfare rights—to education, decent housing, a minimum income or productive work, health care, and other goods that liberal egalitarians deem essential to human dignity in the midst of affluence—have been challenged for a more subtle and significant reason: as the province of rights expands, the territory subject to democratic control contracts. "Rights have this special characteristic: their violation requires immediate relief or reparation. And judges are not merely the available, they are also the appropriate instruments of relief and reparation."[2] There is this logical connection, at least within our political and legal system, between rights and judges. There is also an historical connection between the championship of more civil and political rights by philosophers, political theorists, and law professors, and a period of remarkable judicial activism, which may now be drawing to a close in the United States. This logic and history suggest to democrats like Michael Walzer and John Hart Ely that there is an inverse relationship between the extent of democracy and the egalitarian

I wish to thank Donald Herzog, Douglas MacLean, Claudia Mills, Michael Walzer, and participants in the Yale Legal Theory Seminar for their helpful comments.

extension of liberalism. And so they charge liberal egalitarians with extending to courts an invitation to intrude radically upon what is rightfully democratic authority.[3]

To judge whether liberal egalitarianism radically and wrongly intrudes upon democratic space, we need to establish a standard of what constitutes the proper domain of democratic authority. But were democrats and egalitarians in agreement upon such a standard, this dispute would never arise. So, instead of redefending an ideal egalitarian constitution that recognizes welfare rights along with the value of democratic participation, I try to meet the challenge of democrats who attack welfare rights on their own ground. I want to demonstrate that the constraints upon democracy that they sanction are more intrusive upon democratic space than their attack suggests.

But suppose we concede that an ideal constitution by democratic standards contains more space for democratic decisionmaking than an ideal egalitarian constitution, what follows for our judgment of the relative merits of these two constitutions? The presumption of committed democrats is that democratic experience is clearly more valuable than the welfare rights that would constrain it. In the second part of this essay, I examine several reasons democrats offer in support of this presumption. Their strongest case against the judicial enforcement of welfare rights derives from nonideal theory, or what might be called an argument from tradition. But this argument is no less compatible with an ideal egalitarian theory than it is with an ideal democratic one.

In conclusion, I offer some reasons for questioning the basic premise of the democratic attack upon welfare rights: that there is a clear distinction to be made on the basis of democratic values between legislative decisionmaking and judicial enforcement of constitutional rights.

How Intrusive Are Democratic Constraints?

Even the most committed democrats do not believe that all policies resulting from the process by which popularly elected politicians make laws governing those whom they collectively represent are just. They accept Schumpeter's claim that "we should certainly not approve of . . . practices [of persecuting Christians, burning witches, and slaughtering Jews] on the ground that they have been decided on according to the rule of democratic procedure."[4] But they reject his conclusion that democracy is therefore valuable only as a method of achieving ideals and interests that are themselves not intrinsically democratic. Committed democrats regard democracy as valuable in itself, for reasons I shall explore later, but not so valuable as to sanction gross abuses of justice such as the ones Schumpeter mentions.

They place two constraints upon the democratic process that would condemn such practices and authorize courts to override the will of democratic majorities prepared to engage in such practices.

The first constraint is nondiscrimination: "The people must will generally. They cannot single out (except in elections for public office) a particular individual or set of individuals from among themselves for special treatment."[5] This principle is not uniquely tied to democratic values; it is widely recognized as a necessary condition for any laws to be just.[6] But one might argue, following Rousseau, that the nondiscrimination principle has a special place in democratic theory in obligating minorities to accept majoritarian decisions. "The undertakings which bind us to the social body are obligatory," Rousseau argued, "only because they are mutual."[7] From the requirement of mutuality, Rousseau derived the nondiscrimination constraint: "the general will, to be really such, must be general in its object as well as its essence; . . . it must both come from all and apply to all."[8] John Hart Ely also offers a version of the nondiscrimination constraint, and he claims that the consistency of this constraint "with democratic theory . . . [is] at least as important as the argument from the nature of the Constitution."[9]

The second constraint, against political repression, derives from an understanding of democracy that is also broader than Schumpeter's: democracy requires not merely electoral representation, but a free and fair process of representation over time. The constraint on political repression requires that the processes of political change be structured so as to prevent "the ins [from] choking off the channels of political change to ensure that they will stay in and the outs will stay out."[10] The most effective (and unjust) way of ensuring that the outs will stay out is to persecute and slaughter them. Both nondiscrimination and nonrepression require democrats to condemn such horrendous practices as undemocratic in character. If we accept the committed democrats' understanding of a fair system of representation then the more challenging question is not whether they can avoid sanctioning tyranny by the majority, but whether they can (or should) stop short of sanctioning intrusions upon the legislative will of the majority as great as those for which they criticize liberal egalitarians. To answer this question, we must look more closely at the rationale and political implications of the two democratic constraints.

NONDISCRIMINATION

It is impossible to specify precisely what the prohibition on legal discrimination demands without determining its rationale. Even then it will not be easy. The most general reason for democrats to support a principle that "the people must will generally" is an elementary condition of justice that equals should be treated equally. "There is one principle of distributive justice on which there seems to be general agreement," William Frankena notes, "namely, that like cases or individuals are to be dealt with in the same way or treated alike."[11] In its negative form, the principle rules out laws that make arbitrary distinctions.[12]

But what distinctions are arbitrary? To answer this question, we need some standard of distribution that is not apparently given by the nondiscrimination principle itself. The most plausible standard for a democrat to choose is relevant reasons: laws are arbitrary if they make distinctions among people for reasons that by current social understanding are deemed irrelevant to their entitlement to the good being distributed.[13]

The standard of relevant reasons is attractive from a democratic perspective because, unlike many other principles of justice, its distributive criterion is relative to the dominant social understanding of what constitutes good grounds for distributing a particular good. This relativism is also a source of considerable ambiguity in its practical application. But many cases are clear. For example: democratic majorities may single out particular people (with proper names) to enjoy the benefits of public office but not the benefits of free speech because (in a democratic society) winning an election is considered a relevant reason for enjoying the benefits of the former but not the latter. The nondiscrimination constraint is not violated by a law that provides special educational services designed to aid the mentally handicapped, but it is by one that provides the same services only to mentally handicapped Protestants, Caucasians, or men. Being Protestant, Caucasian, or male is not a relevant grounds for being entitled to special education, while being mentally handicapped is.

These examples illustrate the appeal of the nondiscrimination constraint as well as the difficulty of generalizing about its requirements. If it permits special treatment for the sick and the old, it is probably not because "We can all get sick and we all hope to grow old."[14] Those of us who are fortunate enough not to be born mentally handicapped neither expect nor hope to become so. A law restricting special services to mentally handicapped men need not mention proper names, yet at least in our society it would be as blatant a violation of the generality principle as a law providing the same services only to Protestants. These examples suggest that the nondiscrimination principle may permit courts very broad powers of review over legislation to determine whether the discriminations made between those who benefit from a law and those who do not are justifiable by relevant reasons. Irrelevant discriminations authorize courts to restrict legislative will. The search for a dominant social understanding of relevance opens up a considerable realm for judicial discretion. But this is surely not a sufficient reason for rejecting the relevant reasons constraint upon legislation without a better one to put in its place.

Ely suggests that there is a better and less restrictive version of the nondiscrimination constraint. To the extent that his alternative is less restrictive, however, it is also less defensible. He argues that majoritarian legislation may be overridden when it "systematically disadvantag[es] some minority out of simple hostility or a prejudiced refusal to recognize commonalities of interest, and thereby den[ies] that minority the protection afforded other groups by a representative system."[15] By focusing on legislative motivation, Ely wants to avoid constraining democracy by what he calls "fundamental" values, judgments of the fairness of distributions, which Ely implies are necessarily arbitrary or personal preferences.[16] But surely prejudice against aliens is not a sufficient reason for overriding a law that systematically disadvantages them in relation to citizens (e.g., by granting them only temporary visas for educational purposes). And it is not clear why majoritarian prejudice or hostility should be necessary for a finding of legislative discrimination. Suppose Congress passed a law that guaranteed all men equal pay for equal work. Would the fact that women are not a minority nor (arguably) an object of prejudice or hostility (assume that half of our legislators were women) mean that this law did not unjustly discriminate against women?[17] Surely it discriminates against those women who work and want fair pay for their work. Prejudicial or hostile legislative motivation and minority status often may be keys to explaining why legislatures pass discriminatory laws, but they are neither necessary nor sufficient criteria for a finding of unjust discrimination.

There is, however, a common and somewhat less restrictive interpretation of nondiscrimination that can be defended by distinguishing between legislative acts and omissions.[18] The equal protection standard of the Fourteenth Amendment is sometimes interpreted so as to require positive action by government in order to trigger the protection by judicial constraint. On this interpretation, a democratic government need not provide public education, but if it provides it for some children, it must provide it for all. Once triggered by positive government action, the standard of equal protection leaves open the legislative option of withdrawing the protection entirely rather than providing it for everyone whose interests are similarly affected. *Palmer v. Thompson* is a well-known example of how this version of equal protection works: the Supreme Court permitted the Ciy Council of Jackson, Mississippi, to close its public swimming pools rather than to desegregate them as a federal district court had ordered.[19] But this case does not demonstrate the difference between a relevant reasons standard and the equal protection interpretation of nondiscrimination, and it is understandably hard to find a good case, since democratic legislatures are much less likely to repeal completely the distribution of a good that by a relevant reasons standard demands public distribution. Nor is it a good case to test the difference between democratic and egalitarian constraints on legislation because recreation has yet to achieve the status of a right on any egalitarian's list.

But consider a more commonly defended egalitarian right, to health care. Whereas the logic of relevant reasons dictates that health care be provided on the basis of illness and not according to income, the equal protection version of nondiscrimination demands only that if a government provides health care to one portion of the population, it may be required to justify singling out that portion on the basis of a relevant reason.[20] Once we start wondering about what reasons meet the standard of relevancy in particular cases—consider who the relevant population is for distribution of goods such as special education or obligations such as military conscription—we cannot help but recognize that the nondiscrimination constraint leaves courts with a large area of discretion in reviewing democratic legislation. Perhaps they should apply the least demanding standard of relevancy possible in order to leave the greatest room for democratic choice. But no plausible moral rationale behind the nondiscrimination constraint itself tells courts that, and if it can be defended at all as a necessary constraint upon democratic decisionmaking, it must be defended on some moral grounds. So as long as the legislature decides to distribute some socially valuable good to some people, it may be required by the courts to distribute it more broadly to all those who are similarly situated or who share a similar need, or else not distribute it at all. Therefore courts that aspire to a consistent and thoroughgoing application of the nondiscrimination constraint are likely to find themselves running against the current of judicial restraint even though the constraint is triggered not by a constitutional right to a particular good but only by a right to nondiscrimination or equal protection. Thus, the nondiscrimination constraint, rather narrowly interpreted, invites courts to intrude upon democratic space without ever having to rest their authority upon the substantive rights defended by liberal egalitarian philosophers.

The significant difference that remains in theory between the intrusiveness potentially justifiable by a rule of nondiscrimination and by specific constitutional rights is that under a nondiscrimination constraint, courts must *prevent* legislatures from enacting laws that make irrelevant distinctions among people, but when bound by constitutional rights, courts must *require* legislatures to enact laws to protect them. The nondiscrimination constraint thus leaves legislatures more freedom to decide which goods they and their constituents value most, whereas constitutional rights to specific goods determine priorities for the people rather than by them or their democratic representatives.

Were equal protection the only constraint upon the will of the people sanctioned by democrats, then at least in theory there might be an enormous area of legislative freedom in a democracy that would not exist in a society governed by liberal egalitarian principles. If it so willed, a democratic assembly need not guarantee freedom of speech, religion, or association to any of its citizens nor secure their personal property nor protect them against self-incrimination or ex post facto laws, let alone provide them with health care or education or a minimum income. Although it is very unlikely that any democratic legislature would act (or fail to act) in such a way as to deny all of these goods to those it represents, it is only by virtue of the second constraint upon its authority that legislatures can be required on democratic principle by courts to provide some of them.

NONREPRESSION

The second constraint is really a set of constraints designed to ensure the fairness of the democratic process and therefore to protect democracy from itself. The justification for these constraints (unlike those of nondiscrimination) is specifically democratic: A legislature must provide those goods and respect those rights, but only those goods and rights, necessary for the fair functioning of the democratic process over time. It is essential that democrats require that the process of democracy be fairly constituted because they do not want to permit courts (except insofar as nondiscrimination requires) to constrain the legislation according to its results. Thus Walzer and Ely both reject a third constraint that "the people must will what is right."[21] But if legislative majorities need not will what is right, then they must at least rule minorities rightly.

What does the standard of a fair democratic process require? "Discussions of the meaning of 'democracy,'" Ely tells us, "no matter how scrupulous they are about noting the existence of some variations in understanding, seem invariably to include political equality, or the principle that everyone's vote is to count for the same."[22] But political equality is surely not exhausted by an electoral principle of one person-one vote. As Ely's own sources indicate, for nearly all democratic theorists, political equality means "equal opportunity for every individual to participate in governing."[23] Interpreting equality of political opportunity is not an easy task, but we can take it to mean (roughly) that all individuals who are capable of understanding and obeying laws should have an equal opportunity to participate in making them or electing and influencing the policies of those who make them in their name. This may be a more demanding standard than some democrats have in mind when they criticize liberal egalitarians for being undemocratic. But they have not offered, nor can I find, a less demanding standard that makes sense of the idea that the will of the people as revealed in competitive elections or by their elected representatives in law may not be truly democratic under all conditions.

What are those rights and goods necessary for ensuring equality of political opportunity? The legislature clearly may not deny the right to vote to any individual who is capable of understanding and obeying its laws. This right to vote must be inalienable. Any citizen can choose not to exercise his or her right to vote. But "the people cannot renounce now their future right to will (or, no such renunciation can ever be legitimate or morally effective). Nor can they deny to some group among themselves, with or without a proper name, the right to participate in future willing."[24] Citizens or their representatives may not decide by any procedural rule to create a nondemocratic political system. A decision by a current majority to do so would prevent a new majority next year (which consisted of some citizens who were in the minority on today's vote) from implementing the democratic will. Even a unanimous decision to renounce democracy would be illegitimate because it would bind future generations who would not have the right to choose whether to make democratic choices.

But inalienable universal suffrage is only one among many rights that "guarantee the democratic character of the popular will."[25] If elections are to reflect the popular will in any meaningful sense, then citizens must be informed about the political choices actually and potentially available to them; they must be able to communicate their political opinions effectively among themselves and to their representatives; they must be free to make choices about how to live their own lives that help them determine the law by which they want to be governed. We need not move beyond these rough standards of what is necessary to ensure that the will of the people or their representatives has a democratic character in order to generate a tentatively large set of defensible "democratic rights": to freedom of speech, religion, and association; to education and access to the mass media; to privacy; and to employment or a minimum income (defined by prevailing standards of social acceptability). All of these rights admit of more and less expansive interpretations, but the democratic rationale for them invites courts to expand their interpretations only to the extent necessary to permit citizens the freedom to engage in a fair democratic process.

How extensive should these rights then be? No general answer is available. We need to consider carefully the relationship between each right and the fairness of the democratic process, which is a project beyond the scope of this essay. But let's briefly consider a few examples, beginning with the right most commonly identified as a precondition of democracy, free speech. It is hard to find any category of speech, including pornography, in which a citizen's interest is not relevant to his or her political opinions.[26] The only category of speech that seems to be ruled out of protection on democratic grounds is subliminal communication because it prevents us from discovering and therefore evaluating the reason for our personal or political preferences.[27] There are types of pornography that we might argue are not relevant to the formation of political opinions, but we must then ask whether legislatures, rather than courts, should be trusted to distinguish between speech that is and is not of redeeming political value. Given the immediate interest that legislators have in stifling speech that conflicts with their own political views, it is hard to argue on democratic grounds that judges should defer to legislative opinion when a law is challenged as violating free speech.[28]

The democratic value of the freedom to form political opinions is sufficiently great to permit courts to override the legislative will when they have reason to believe that it interferes with that freedom. My tentative conclusion therefore is that the democratic rationale for free speech supports a right about as extensive as one would support on liberal grounds of individual autonomy.[29] The democratic right of free speech thus invites courts to impose their deliberative will upon that of legislative assemblies in the name of the people whom those legislators claim to represent. In the case of a right to free speech, the equation used to criticize egalitarians—"The more rights the judges award to the people as individuals, the less free the people are as a decisionmaking body"—is misleading.[30] Legislators are not the only people in a democracy who make decisions collectively. So do voters, and their freedom to make a collective decision at the polls is increased by the free speech rights judges award to them as individuals, although the freedom of their elected representatives is at the same time restricted.

But democrats are more likely to contest some of the other candidates for democratic rights on my tentative list: the rights to education and employment or a minimum income are among the most obvious targets. If they concede that these are democratic rights, they will want to specify them narrowly enough to prevent courts from re-stricting the legislative will more than the democratic process requires.

The first question is whether democrats must concede that these rights, even quite narrowly construed, are necessary to guarantee a fair democratic process or equality of political opportunity. If political equality requires only that there be competitive elections and delib-erative procedures within legislatures—that is, if no requirements guarantee that all citizens are sufficiently educated to understand and to participate in politics—then it is hard to understand why anyone would value the democratic process so highly as to subordinate all nondemocratic values to its authority. Those theorists who have defined the democratic standard minimally—to take a classic example, as an "institutional arrangement for arriving at political decisions in which individuals acquire the power to decide by means of a competitive struggle for the people's vote"[31]—have not valued the democratic process above those ultimate ends like justice with which its results may conflict.

Anyone with a higher evaluation of democracy must also have a more demanding standard than Schumpeter's for assessing the democratic character of the popular will. Let's assume committed democrats like Walzer accept my standard of a fair democratic process, one of equal opportunity for citizens to participate in influencing the outcome of competitive elections and the policies that their representatives support.[32] Assuming acceptance of this standard, must democrats support rights to education and employment or a minimum income? Surely, without a primary education for basic literacy, American citizens would not be capable of making informed choices during elections or carrying on the deliberative activities of politics between elections. For democratic politics to be a valuable (or potentially valuable) part of our lives, we need to be provided with at least enough education to understand the political choices available to us and to appreciate the value of the collective deliberative activity itself. In addition, an ignorant and illiterate electorate is unlikely to be able to influence the policies of its representatives or to hold them accountable to its preferences. An uneducated citizenry affords the greatest opportunity for manipulation and deception in democratic politics. By the standard of fair democratic process, we can conclude that any American citizens who are denied a basic education will not have an equal opportunity to participate in politics, and are therefore being denied one of their democratic rights.

Something similar might be said about the denial of employment or a minimal income. The connection between these goods and democratic opportunity is less direct, but no less significant. Without guaranteed employment or income, there will be an underclass of poor and unemployed citizens. These citizens will be at the mercy of anyone willing to pay them anything to do virtually anything. Democratic politicians may of course seek the support of this group of citizens, by virtue of their sheer numbers. But, for a variety of reasons connected to their economic dependency, politicians will not have to support the interests of the poor to gain their votes. The lack of civil independence of the poor and unemployed all but binds them to political dependency (as Kant recognized in another context). In addition, the condition of poverty and unemployment in a society that does not recognize a citizen's right to a job or a minimum income makes the job of educating the children of this underclass all but impossible. The expectation that one will remain poor and unemployed is a powerful disincentive to taking public education seriously.

But the claim that all citizens—young and old—have a democratic right to a basic education and employment or a minimum income raises a serious problem for democratic theorists, one that is commonly cited by critics of welfare rights.[33] Why should a relatively small proportion of citizens have a right to demand that government spend a disproportionally large amount of its resources in meeting their needs? What if recognizing these democratic rights forces legislators to neglect other needs and preferences of a majority of their constituents on the grounds that the needs of the poor are the most urgent? Would judicial enforcement of a right to employment on democratic grounds just be a more subtle form of the tyranny of minorities over the will of majorities?

Judicial enforcement of the rights to education and employment or a minimum income certainly would have the effect of seriously restricting legislative choice. Legislatures could still choose *how* to fulfill these rights: for example, what kind of jobs to create or how much income constitutes a socially acceptable minimum. But whatever policies the legislature chooses, the rights to education and employment or a minimum income are bound to cost a lot of money and restrict choice among other goods desired by more citizens.[34]

What should we conclude from the fact that recognition of even a short list of welfare rights intrudes deeply upon democratic or at least legislative space? We must choose among three alternatives: (1) the standard of a fair democratic process is too demanding; (2) even a short list of welfare rights is longer than necessary for satisfying the democratic standard; or (3) some significant limits upon democratic space are necessary and legitimate. My arguments have pointed in the direction of the third conclusion. Until democrats offer a less demanding but more defensible standard of democratic fairness and provide reasons why these qualified rights to education, employment, or income are not necessary to satisfy that standard, our most reasonable conclusion is that the constraints of nondiscrimination and nonrepression, taken singly and (even more so) together, invite "judicial activity that is radically intrusive on what might be called democratic space."[35]

We must also recognize that more radical intrusions are possible, as the list of rights defended by some egalitarian philosophers indicates. A right of equal access to health care, for example, restricts the legislative will much more than the democratic right to basic education, employment, or a minimum income. Philosophers defending this unqualified right to health care may encourage courts to apply the most expansive interpretation of that right that can be defended constitutionally and philosophically.[36] The same can be said regarding the rights to education, welfare, meaningful work, and privacy justified by some egalitarian principles. Like the right to free speech, these rights admit of judicial interpretations that are more or less restrictive of legislative will. But unlike the right to free speech, the standard of a fair democratic process does not clearly require a broad interpretation of these rights (or arguably recognition of any right at all).

So, the ideal constitution of many liberal egalitarians would sanction greater intrusions upon democratic space than the ideal constitution of committed democrats. But this does not mean that liberal egalitarianism sanctions more judicial intervention under our present (nonideal) Constitution. How much judicial intervention is justified by liberal egalitarianism depends upon how our present Constitution should be interpreted and what role courts should play in moving us toward a more ideal constitution. Unless our Constitution can be reasonably interpreted as supporting welfare rights, liberal egalitarians need not and probably should not sanction judicial intervention based upon those rights.[37] This is an important qualification upon the claim that liberal egalitarians invite radically intrusive judicial activity, because no liberal egalitarian that I know of is committed to the view that judges should make their decisions based upon the demands of justice alone regardless of the language of the Constitution or law that they are authorized to interpret.

Ronald Dworkin, for example, argues for judicial interventionism insofar as constitutional language and legal precedent support the rights that he takes seriously as a moral philosopher.[38] Ely interprets some of the same constitutional language to sanction only those interventions required by something similar to the two democratic constraints. But the very nature of their arguments suggests that a philosophical defense of rights does not suffice to justify judicial interventionism. I shall return to explore the practical implications of this point in conclusion.

Although we might question in more detail how far the two democratic constraints taken together move us toward the rights that many liberal egalitarians defend, I want to admit for the sake of further argument that liberal egalitarian rights have the potential for justifying more extensive judicial incursions upon legislative space than do the two democratic constraints. So now we must ask: How troubled should liberal egalitarians be by this admission?

Is Democracy More Valuable Than Liberal Rights?

A philosophical defense of any rights that are not uncontroversially preconditions of fair democratic process raises this question, relevant to our opinion of judicial activism in school desegregation, prison and welfare reform, and the ideology and programs of the "new federalism."

In claiming that "welfare rights would radically reduce the reach of democratic decision," Walzer implies that this is on balance a bad thing.[39] But why should we believe that a reduction in the reach of collective decisionmaking is a loss that outweighs the corresponding gain in the welfare of individual citizens?

MORAL SKEPTICISM

Three reasons are often given or implied by democratic theorists. The first—perhaps the most commonly offered in popular political discourse and relied upon by Ely in his attack upon the "fundamental values" approach to constitutional interpretation—is that substantive rights are just reflections of the personal values of judges and therefore have no moral standing against the popular will of majorities.[40] While the other arguments provide reasons for valuing democracy, based upon the democratic experience and tradition, this one rests on our inability to ground rights philosophically and hence to give them moral weight *against* democracy. To the other arguments I shall respond that while democratic experience and tradition are indeed quite valuable, they are not valuable enough to override every other important human interest. But this argument, if accepted, pulls the moral rug out from under philosophers who would wish to defend certain substantive rights against democracy. Perhaps this explains its great attraction to committed democrats.

As many critics of Ely have pointed out, the knockdown quality of the argument from moral skepticism is also destructive of the democrat's own case.[41] It applies with equal force against our ability to ascribe moral value to the democratic process and the rights necessary to support that process. Either democratic and liberal rights in principle can both be valuable or neither can. While the latter always remains a theoretical possibility, we must simply ignore it in order to speak or to act with moral reason as committed democrats or liberal egalitarians. So I shall leave the argument from moral skepticism behind and concentrate on the other two.

DEMOCRATIC EXPERIENCE

The second argument is that "the [democratic] experience itself, the process through which the products [of legislation are] produced," is a very valuable part of the life of a democratic citizen.[42] Democrats like Walzer who are not moral skeptics claim that the value of democratic participation is too great to be subordinated to the value of being governed by just laws that are not democratically enacted. This language may be confusing because it permits us to say that democratic majorities have the right to rule unjustly. It is not inconsistent, however, for a democrat to claim that because democratic participation is a morally valuable good, majorities should have the right to pass laws that are not just (in content) so long as they are justly (i.e., democratically) enacted. To clarify this position, we might distinguish between the legitimacy and justice of a law, and settle for saying that democratically enacted laws can be legitimate without being just. Conversely, laws governing the distribution of goods other than political power can be just without being legitimately enacted; e.g., if courts override legislative will without having the legitimate authority (by democratic standards) to do so.

According to democrats, any law governing the distribution of a good passed by the assembled people or their political representatives that does not violate the two democratic prohibitions on discrimination and political repression is legitimate. The courts have no authority to override a democratic decision in the name of an individual's or group's right to a share of the good in question. But why should the process by which such a law is enacted suffice to determine its legitimacy when an important good—such as education, income, or health care—is at stake? Is the democratic experience either ideally or in practice today so valuable as to deny courts any authority to constrain legislatures when they fail to provide citizens with access to these goods?

There are two important truths in the democrat's defense of political participation and attack upon judicial authority. The right to participate as an equal in democratic politics is a particularly important interest of citizens in any society committed to the idea of human equality, and that right is meaningful only if democratic decisionmaking is not authoritatively constrained in every instance by an elite institution. The second truth follows closely from the first: The people or their representatives acting democratically need not always will what is right for their will to become the authoritative law governing their society. Liberal philosophers whose lists of rights exhaust the valuable goods available for social distribution fail to appreciate the combined force of these truths: that the good of egalitarian distribution of political power cannot simply be subordinated to the egalitarian distribution of nonpolitical goods without forsaking the ideal of political equality to which both liberals and democrats are committed.

But these are only partial truths, which do not lead directly to the sweeping conclusion that the distributive or "redistributive pattern [the people] choose is not [and should not be] subject to authoritative correction in accordance with philosophical standards."[43] Nor to the conclusion that "the people would . . . be ill-advised to agree to [incorporate a right to welfare into their constitution] and to surrender so large a part of their day-to-day authority."[44] At this point in the democratic argument we must ask whether the opportunity to guarantee themselves and their children a right to health care, decent housing, a minimum income, and a more than minimal education would not be worth the additional constraint upon their legislative authority?

In a direct democracy, the answer might, arguably, be "no." Public activity occupies so great a portion of the lives of citizens that their individual welfare may be less important.[45] If a minority seeks health care or decent housing through judicial intervention, satisfying their interests by placing far-reaching constitutional constraints upon the popular will might be too great a price to pay in a society where democratic participation is so valuable. I say "might" because it is not clear that the balance of goods tips in the direction of democratic experience even in a society where that experience constitutes a central and valuable portion of the lives of most citizens.

But the argument from democratic experience faces a possibly insurmountable obstacle erected by the nature of political participation in representative democracies. In representative democracies, the people do not assemble to give the laws to themselves. This may be the best form of government practicable in modern societies, but it prevents us from transferring Rousseau's claims for the value of democracy directly to our own experience. "In a well-ordered city every man flies to the assemblies."[46] In a direct democracy, the private affairs of citizens are of relatively little importance, because political life furnishes such a great proportion of the happiness of each individual, "that there is less for him to seek in particular cares."[47]

In a representative democracy, citizens stay at home while their elected representatives make laws. The private affairs of citizens are of relatively great importance, in part because the common experience of political participation furnishes a very small proportion of the satisfactions of each individual so that there is a great deal left for men and women to seek in particular cares. Once citizens are not invited to fly to political assemblies, to debate and cast their votes on particular pieces of legislation, why should they prefer (and why should philosophers advise them to prefer) greater legislative discretion for their representatives to a more just distribution of goods conducive to individual welfare?

Every loss in the authoritative control of a representative assembly over legislation cannot be translated into an equally great loss in control by the people in making their own laws, since the people begin with direct control only over choosing their representatives. The political processes of existing representative democracies certainly do not afford effective means of communicating the majority's preferences on particular issues, let alone ensuring that those preferences become law. The mass media offer a means of political communication affordable only by the few who are rich. The many who are not must bear the additional cost of organizing to communicate their views. This is not an argument for maximizing judicial over legislative authority, but merely for clarifying whether our evaluation of the democratic experience is based upon the reality of American representative democracy, ideal representative democracy, or the clearly unattainable (and perhaps for other reasons undesirable) ideal of direct democracy.[48]

The satisfactions that Rousseau ascribes to political participation in a direct democracy may provide us with reasons for trying to increase the incentives for and the value of political participation in a representative democracy. But any attempt to make political participation a more valued part of the lives of American citizens is likely to require restructuring political institutions and redistributing social goods in the face of legislative opposition, a problem of restricting democracy in order to revive it that committed democrats seem too eager to avoid.

The costs of avoiding the problem are great. Not only do democrats ascribe unrealistically high value to the democratic experience of the average American citizen, they also neglect to consider the much lower value that the experience has for economically disadvantaged citizens who more often than not find themselves an ineffectual minority on redistributive issues. The second constraint against political repression gives democrats a way of handling this problem. A qualified right to welfare "would guarantee to each citizen the opportunity to exercise his citizenship, and that is an opportunity he could hardly be said to have, or to have in any meaningful fashion, if he were starving to death or desperately seeking shelter for himself and his family."[49]

While remaining on their own ground, therefore, democratic theorists can defend some of the same welfare rights as liberal egalitarians. At the same time democratic fairness provides a plausible standard, lacking within most liberal egalitarian theories, by which to set limits upon the otherwise unlimited resource demands and intrusiveness of many welfare rights, such as the right of "equal access to health care" or "equal educational opportunity."[50] Democrats can support these rights insofar as they support a reasonable standard of equal political opportunity. They also can prevent "judicial hijacking" of legislative decisionmaking by limiting the court's authority to enforcing only those rights to health care or education that clearly are necessary to political opportunity.

This limit will be difficult to determine, even under the best constitutions. But to resist entirely the move toward recognizing some welfare rights on grounds that judicial enforcement would radically reduce the value of the democratic experience is to ignore the negligible value of that experience for those citizens who suffer from the willful or benign neglect of democratic majorities. If we accept the argument from democratic experience as sufficient to override all welfare rights, we must be prepared to claim that it is worth sacrificing both political equality and the welfare interests of minorities in order to increase the scope of the democratic experience. Can democrats make good on this claim? Probably not, but I am concerned here only to establish the form that the democratic argument against welfare rights must take if it is based only on the value of the participatory experience itself. I leave an assessment of the validity of this argument in particular cases for another time.

THE ARGUMENT FROM TRADITION

A third argument against judicial activism, or as Walzer puts it, a worry democratic citizens might have about courts enforcing rights against democratic decisions, is that it "will involve overriding their own traditions, conventions, and expectations."[51] Of course, an argument against disturbing a society's traditions, conventions, and expectations need not be a democratic argument since the political traditions of most societies are not democratic. But there is much to be said for respecting an established political tradition that appears to have the widespread support of its people. There is an unfortunate tendency among political philosophers to weigh traditions and conventions absolutely or not at all. Since the conventional political practices of modern societies are never universally supported by their members, those practices are always open to philosophical criticism even on internal grounds, that the interests and beliefs of some members are being systematically neglected or overridden. And because some of the social practices and institutions of all but the most inhumane regimes are valuable as tradition, some moral weight should be given to tradition against the application of ideal principles to particular societies or in the very construction of those principles that are to guide evaluations of a society and recommendations for institutional change.

But the major problem in defending democracy in America against liberalism on grounds of tradition is that the defense begs the question under dispute. What is at issue is not simply which rights against democracy are philosophically justifiable in light of our democratic tradition, but what that tradition is. How democratic are our Constitution and the political conventions and expectations it has created over time?[52] The same philosophers who challenge the relative value of democratic procedures in light of certain welfare rights on moral grounds can also challenge the democratic interpretation of our political tradition on historical and constitutional grounds. The debate between Ely and most of his critics is one of constitutional interpretation as well as moral philosophy. This debate attests to the difficulty, even if not the impossibility, of separating the two enterprises. At least in the case of the argument between committed democrats and liberal egalitarians, there is not enough in the text of the Constitution, our constitutional history, and widely accepted judicial precedents to support either interpretation on constitutional grounds alone.

One can say with confidence on grounds of constitutional tradition alone that we have inherited a mixed political system. In our tradition of liberal democratic government the will of the people as expressed through representative legislatures and an executive (neither of which is elected on a purely majoritarian basis) is constrained constitutionally both by procedural rules governing these institutions and also by substantive rights that are not solely or mainly derived from the requirements of a fair democratic process, rights such as freedom of religion and "the right of the people to be secure in their persons, houses, papers, and effects," which are therefore enforceable by the courts.

If American citizens today resent judicial incursions upon legislative will, is it because political tradition has led them to expect more judicial restraint? Take the cases of judicial activism that are criticized most often by conservatives and unreconstructed democrats, the school desegregration cases following the *Brown* decisions. Is it the people's legitimate expectations based upon their democratic traditions and conventions that are violated by these decisions or their present, intense opposition to busing and other "involuntary" means of school integration? If it is only the latter (it could of course be both), the argument from tradition surely carries no weight because constitutional rights were intended by our political tradition to secure important interests of individuals against the excesses of popular, even intense popular, will.

I am not prepared here to argue that popular opposition to judicially enforced busing or other welfare rights is grounded only upon an intense conflict of interests and not upon violation of constitutional tradition. This is (in part) a question of constitutional interpretation, which deserves careful consideration in its own right. But any argument against judicial activism based upon tradition would have to take account of our constitutional doctrine of mixed, liberal democratic government and ask whether these decisions (or ones based upon welfare rights derived from the equal protection or due process clauses) overstep the boundaries of legitimate expectations set by that tradition. I suspect that, on grounds of constitutional interpretation alone, our political tradition looks neither as democratic and procedural as Ely argues and Walzer's critique of judicial activism implies, nor as liberal and substantively egalitarian as Dworkin and other constitutional theorists sometimes seem to suggest.[53] But I do not think that the debate between unreconstructed democrats and liberal egalitarians is best focused on constitutional interpretations, since these have changed over time, as have our moral principles. In addition, changing social and economic circumstances sometimes require a different understanding of constitutional rights even when our moral principles remain constant. Within the limits of reasonable interpretations of constitutional language and intent, we probably have no better choice than to recognize the dependence of constitutional interpretation upon political philosophy.

But suppose we discover that there are judicial decisions based upon unreasonable interpretation of constitutional language, where no constitutional provision plausibly can be taken to support a particular welfare right. Democratic theorists criticize liberal egalitarians for inviting courts to enforce the welfare rights that they defend philosophically. But a philosophical defense of welfare rights, which assumes an ideal constitution, surely need not authorize judicial enforcement of those rights under a nonideal democratic constitution any more than democratic principles would authorize courts to refuse to enforce welfare rights under a liberal egalitarian constitution. Where a constitution is silent or speaks clearly against certain rights, so must judges, whether they are democrats or liberal egalitarians. So, the most cogent argument against judicial intervention, based on democratic tradition—that courts should not be freed from the constraints of constitutionalism—is neutral between democratic and liberal egalitarian theories of justice. Of course, our Constitution rarely speaks clearly on these issues, in which cases liberal egalitarian judges may intrude more upon legislative will in defending more extensive rights to welfare than those who are committed democrats. But under these nonideal circumstances, it is not clear how judges can, or why they should, ignore principles of justice in interpreting the Constitution.

THE CONSEQUENCES OF DEMOCRATIC DECISIONMAKING

Moral skepticism, the value of democratic experience, and tradition surely do not exhaust the reasons we might have for defending democratic decisionmaking against judicial enforcement of liberal rights. But if we pose the problem as whether to support legislative or judicial authority in a representative democracy if the former systematically violates and the latter reliably upholds principles of distributive justice, then tradition may be the best defense of legislative against judicial authority. This misrepresents, however, the nature of the problems generally facing representative democracies at the same time as it unrealistically skews the argument in favor of judicial authority.

Why assume that courts will use their authority more justly than legislatures? This assumption may help test how dependent our commitment to democracy is upon the results of the democratic process. But even if it is very dependent upon consequences, we should not assume that it is therefore weak.[54] Not all rights that liberals have traditionally supported and certainly not all constitutional rights are based upon just distributive principles, and few constitutional rights can be stated so precisely as to preclude interpretations that are incompatible with principles of justice. Consider the right to property stated in the Fifth Amendment and supported by many liberals: "nor shall any person . . . be deprived of . . . property, without due process of law; nor shall private property be taken for public use, without just compensation." A liberal egalitarian would have a hard time arguing that the constitutional right to property has brought us closer to a just society than we would have been had legislatures early in this century been freer to pass laws regulating property.

On the other hand, the right to religious freedom has brought us closer to a just society and has no doubt been better protected as a constitutional right than it otherwise would have been. It is a right that liberal egalitarians defend, and defend more persuasively on liberal rather than democratic grounds. The right to education included in many state constitutions seems to have brought us closer to a just society by protecting the interests of children against undue neglect by legislative majorities. Although it has been interpreted quite broadly by some state courts, judicial constraints on the distribution of education have not eroded legislative energy or the political interest of local communities in their children's education.

Why then assume away the obvious facts that rights are not equally valuable nor courts reliably just when we consider the relative value of democratic and judicial authority? An argument for democratic authority based upon judging the consequences of allocating authority between legislatures and courts does not preclude consideration of the value of democratic experience and tradition, but it focuses upon a more common appreciation of democratic authority among citizens: its relatively greater responsiveness than elite institutions to their interests and preferences. But this consequentialist argument leaves open the possibility of sanctioning judicial authority for categories of cases where legislatures are more likely to be unjust than are courts by, for example, disregarding essential interests of minorities.

Another, more generally applicable consequentialist consideration is the effect of democratic authority in educating citizens in politics and hence increasing their vigilance against tyranny.[55] It is hard to know how to weigh this consideration in cases where our choice is between legislative injustice and judicial justice, but it at least establishes a strong general presumption in favor of legislative authority. As I suggested earlier, our choice in practice can rarely be so simply stated as between democratic injustice and judicial justice.

Conclusion: Narrowing the Grounds for Criticism

The distinct language of democratic theory and liberal egalitarianism masks a good deal of commonality in the requirements of their ideal constitutions. Perhaps an ideal democratic constitution would enumerate fewer specific rights than a liberal egalitarian one, but it would effectively protect many of the same rights by prohibiting legislation that arbitrarily discriminates between majorities and minorities or undermines the democratic ideal of political equality. Which theory provides a better rationale for constraining legislative decisionmaking may still be an interesting issue, but perhaps less consequential than the terms of the ongoing debate between committed democrats and egalitarians imply. I have therefore focused instead on what might be considered a prior issue: determining the extent to which the political consequences of liberal egalitarianism and democratic principles are bound to differ in societies governed by their respectively ideal constitutions.

While I certainly have not resolved the conflict in ideal theory between committed democrats and liberal egalitarians, I want to suggest on the basis of the previous discussion that this conflict is, or at least should be, relatively contained in its practical application to contemporary American politics. On the level of ideal theory, my argument can be summarized as follows: If some justifiable rights are not conditions of *democratic* fairness, then in order to determine whether those rights should be judicially enforced, we should consider the relative likelihood that courts as compared with legislatures will enforce them. If and only if the likelihood of judicial enforcement seems greater, we must balance the value of attaining these rights against the value of the democratic experience that would be restricted by virtue of that attainment.

But under what practical circumstances will liberal rights and democratic authority actually conflict so as to require this difficult process of balancing?

Not when the Constitution and existing laws are silent. Where no constitutional language can plausibly be interpreted to support a particular welfare right, then liberals must agree with democrats that courts have no authority to enforce that right. Here a version of the argument from tradition holds sway against the judicial enforcement of egalitarian principles.

Not when the Constitution speaks explicitly in favor of a particular welfare right, say, the right to decent housing. Democrats cannot then argue against judicial authority to enforce that specified constitutional right. Here the argument from tradition works in the opposite direction.

When the constitutional language that supports a right is vague, as it is in the due process and equal protection clauses, leaving room for courts to defend narrow or broad interpretations of the right. Here is the most fertile ground for the conflict between democrats and liberals, although I have suggested that this ground might be greatly reduced by careful examination of the two democratic constraints against legal discrimination and political repression.

When citizens pressure their representatives to pass a constitutional amendment supporting a welfare right. I am not sure that there is a conflict here, although Walzer thinks that philosophers should not advise citizens to amend their constitution to incorporate welfare rights because they thereby surrender too much of their day-to-day political authority.[56] But democrats should not neglect the fact that the amending process tends to engage more citizens more intensely in democratic politics than day-to-day legislation.

Given that many laws are passed with little or no legislative deliberation and also are difficult to repeal, it is not clear why constitutional amendments passed by qualified majorities should be considered less legitimate by democratic standards than ordinary legislation.[57] In fact, all laws, like amendments, bind citizens and legislators who could not take part in making them. The rule of qualified majorities makes amendments more difficult than laws to repeal, but it also encourages more serious debate and more extensive participation in passing them in the first place.

I conclude that a fuller recognition by committed democrats of the rationale and implications of their own principles would go far toward narrowing the grounds of conflict between democracy and egalitarianism in both ideal and nonideal contexts. Democrats have made their case against the defense of welfare rights by egalitarians too easy by neglecting the extent to which their own nondiscrimination and nonrepression principles constrain legislative will and by failing to ask *why* more democracy is preferable to more welfare. Although I have put only democratic theory on the defensive in this essay, a similarly critical examination of the internal logic and implications of liberal egalitarianism would, I think, narrow the conflict still further. In particular, one might press egalitarians to define welfare rights clearly enough to avoid the problem, to which I referred only briefly above, of hijacking social resources and democratic decisionmaking.

So, it may not be undemocratic nor threaten the future value of democracy for liberal egalitarians to encourage citizens to incorporate more welfare rights into their constitution by democratic means. And once explicitly incorporated, courts would have democratic authority to enforce those rights against legislative encroachment. Of course, judges then face the problem of interpreting those constitutional rights, just as governmental bureaucrats face the problem of interpreting legislation before applying it. But I have argued that there is no compelling reason on democratic grounds for judges as a rule to choose the narrowest interpretation of a right rather than the morally best one. The conflicts that thereby arise between liberals and democrats over what constitutes the morally best interpretation of a right are, I have argued, impossible to resolve merely on general principle and will no doubt sometimes be extremely difficult to resolve in practice. I have also tried to show that some of these conflicts—between the value of democratic experience and the preconditions of a fair democratic process or between the weight of tradition and the demands of democratic principles—reappear within the democratic ideal itself. Even if democrats did not have the example of liberal egalitarian philosophers to criticize for being undemocratic, they would have to defend the unconstrained democratic process against some of their own democratic principles. I doubt that they would always succeed in this task. But their defense would be theoretically and politically enlightening for democrats and egalitarians alike.[58]

Notes

1. Liberal rights are inadequate protection against tyranny, but their defense in this context need only rely upon an argument that tyranny would be worse without rights. For a critical examination of alternative ways of defending against tyranny and their inadequacy, see James S. Fishkin, *Tyranny and Legitimacy* (Baltimore: Johns Hopkins University Press, 1979).

2. Michael Walzer, "Philosophy and Democracy," *Political Theory* 9, no. 3 (August 1981): 390.

3. Ibid., p. 391.

4. Joseph A. Schumpeter, *Capitalism, Socialism and Democracy* (London: George Allen & Unwin, 1970), p. 242.

5. Walzer, "Philosophy and Democracy," p. 384.

6. See, e.g., Ch. Perelman, *Justice* (New York: Random House, 1967), pp. 54, 86; and William K. Frankena, "Some Beliefs About Justice," in *Philosophy of Law*, edited by Joel Feinberg and Hyman Gross (Encino and Belmont, Ca.: Dickinson Publishing Co., 1975), pp. 250–58; and S. I. Benn and R. S. Peters, *The Principles of Political Thought* (New York: The Free Press, 1959), p. 148.

7. *The Social Contract*, bk. II, ch. IV.

8. Ibid.

9. John Hart Ely, *Democracy and Distrust* (Cambridge: Harvard University Press, 1980), p. 89. Throughout this essay, I therefore take the liberty to interpret Ely's argument as resting upon democratic theory, and not just upon constitutional interpretation (narrowly understood). I think this is the most consistent meaning, if not the intent, of Ely's work.

10. Ibid., p. 103.

11. Frankena, "Some Beliefs About Justice," p. 250.

12. Benn and Peters, *The Principles of Political Thought*, pp. 131–32; and Perelman, *Justice*, p. 86.

13. For a defense of grounding distributive principles on relevant reasons, see Bernard A. O. Williams, "The Idea of Equality," in *Justice and Equality*, edited by Hugo A. Bedau (Englewood Cliffs, N.J.: Prentice-Hall, 1971), pp. 116–37. Walzer's argument in "In Defense of Equality," *Dissent* (Fall 1973): 399–408, relies upon this form of reasoning. I have critically examined the philosophical status of the logic of relevant reasons in *Liberal Equality* (New York: Cambridge University Press, 1981), pp. 96–118.

14. Walzer, "Philosophy and Democracy," p. 384.

15. Ely, *Democracy and Distrust*, p. 103.

16. Ibid., pp. 43–72 and passim. On p. 54, e.g., Ely argues that: "Our society does not, rightly does not, accept the notion of a discoverable and objectively valid set of moral principles, at least not a set that could plausibly serve to overturn the decisions of our elected representatives."

17. Cf. ibid., pp. 166–70. Ely may be right "in supposing that because women now are in a position to protect themselves they will, [and] that we are thus unlikely to see in the future the sort of official gender discrimination that has marked our past" (p. 169). But the accuracy of this prediction does not establish his criterion for nondiscrimination. It neglects to account for the injustice of a *majority of women* deciding not to protect the essential interests of a minority.

18. I leave open the question of whether this distinction is defensible.

19. 403 U.S. 217 (1971). For a critical discussion of the majority's opinion, see Lawrence H. Tribe, *The Constitutional Protection of Individual Rights* (Mineola, N.Y.: The Foundation Press, 1978), p. 1027. There is, of course, a vast legal literature on the subject of how courts have interpreted and should interpret the equal protection clause, when it is triggered, what it requires. Ely and Tribe represent two significantly different approaches, which might be viewed as corresponding (respectively) to democratic and liberal egalitarian theories of constitutional interpretation. See Ely, *Democracy and Distrust*, pp. 116–36 and Tribe, *Constitutional Protection*, pp. 991–1136.

20. See Williams, "The Idea of Equality," pp. 128–29.

21. See Walzer, "Philosophy and Democracy," p. 384. For the source of this constraint, see Rousseau, *The Social Contract*, bk. II, ch. III.

22. Ely, *Democracy and Distrust*, p. 122.

23. Martin Shapiro, *Law and Politics in the Supreme Court* (New York: The Free Press, 1964), p. 219, quoted in Ely, *Democracy and Distrust*, p. 237, n. 54. See also Philip Green and Robert Dahl, "What is Political Equality?" *Dissent* (Summer 1979): 351–68; and Dahl, "Procedural Democracy" in *Philosophy, Politics and Society*, Fifth Series, edited by Peter Laslett and James Fishkin (New Haven: Yale University Press, 1979), pp. 97–133.

24. Walzer, "Philosophy and Democracy," p. 384.

25. Ibid., p. 384. For a discussion of more general socioeconomic conditions of democracy, see J. Roland Pennock, *Democratic Political Theory* (Princeton: Princeton University Press, 1979), pp. 206–59.

26. I follow here T. M. Scanlon, Jr.'s major contribution to a theory of free speech in "Freedom of Expression and Categories of Expression," *University of Pittsburgh Law Review* 40 (1979): 519–50. Cf. Alexander Meiklejohn, *Political Freedom* (New York: Harper and Row, 1960).

27. Scanlon, "Freedom of Expression," pp. 525–26, 548–49.

28. See ibid., pp. 537ff.

29. Ely's defense of a standard of "strict review" for cases involving free expression supports my conclusion. See *Democracy and Distrust*, pp. 107–16.

30. Walzer, "Philosophy and Democracy," p. 391.

31. Schumpeter, *Capitalism, Socialism and Democracy*, p. 269.

32. Walzer indicates in "Philosophy and Democracy," p. 391, that he does not accept this standard, but he does not try to defend his high evaluation of the democratic experience for all citizens in light of the potential unfairness of the process itself.

33. See, e.g., Charles Fried, "Health Care, Cost Containment, Liberty," Paper delivered to the Institute of Society, Ethics and the Life Sciences, Hastings-on-Hudson, N.Y., October 1979; and Loren E. Lomasky, "Medical Progress and National Health Care," *Philosophy & Public Affairs* 10, no. 1 (Winter 1981): 65–88.

34. For the history of government provision of dialysis in this country, see Richard A. Rettig, "The Policy Debate on Patient Care Financing for Victims of End-Stage Renal Disease," *Law and Contemporary Problems* 40, no. 4 (Autumn 1976): 196–230.

35. Walzer, "Philosophy and Democracy," p. 391.

36. For a defense of that right in its most expansive form, see R. M. Veatch, "What Is a 'Just' Health Care Delivery?," in *Ethics and Health Policy*, edited by R. M. Veatch

and R. Branson (Cambridge, Mass.: Ballinger, 1976), pp. 127–53. Cf. Amy Gutmann, "For and Against Equal Access to Health Care," *Milbank Memorial Fund Quarterly* 59, no. 4 (Fall 1981): 542–60.

37. Of course, this leaves unanswered the question of what are the standards of a reasonable constitutional interpretation. See Owen Fiss, "The Forms of Justice," *Harvard Law Review* 93, no. 1 (November 1979): 1–58. Fiss defends an appropriately constrained form of judicial activism, whose purpose is to give "concrete meaning" to public values and "harmonize [them] with the general structure of the Constitution" (p. 11). For a more general philosophical statement of "conservative justice," see Henry Sidgwick, *The Methods of Ethics*, 7th ed. (London: Macmillan, 1907), bk. III, ch. 5, sec. 3, pp. 271–74, and sec. 7, pp. 293–94. See also Joel Feinberg, "Duty and Obligation in the Non-Ideal World," *Journal of Philosophy* 70 (May 10, 1973): 263–75.

38. Ronald Dworkin, *Taking Rights Seriously* (Cambridge: Harvard University Press, 1977).

39. Walzer, "Philosophy and Democracy," p. 391.

40. Ely, *Democracy and Distrust*, pp. 43–72. See esp. p. 54.

41. See, e.g., Lawrence H. Tribe, "The Puzzling Persistence of Process-Based Constitutional Theories," *Yale Law Journal* 89, no. 6 (May 1980): 1063–79; and C. Edwin Baker, "Neutrality, Process, and Rationality: Flawed Interpretations of Equal Protection," *Texas Law Review* 58, no. 6 (August 1980): 1038–49; and Mark Tushnet, "Darkness on the Edge of Town: The Contributions of John Hart Ely to Constitutional Theory," *Yale Law Journal* 89, no. 6 (May 1980): 1037–62.

42. Walzer, "Philosophy and Democracy," p. 395.

43. Ibid., p. 385.

44. Ibid., p. 392.

45. This is part of Rousseau's description of the life of citizens in a direct democracy in bk. III of *The Social Contract*. But he does not conclude that therefore constraints on the democratic process in the name of distributive fairness are illegitimate.

46. Ibid., bk. III, ch. XV.

47. Ibid.

48. For doubts about the desirability of direct democracy, see Jane J. Mansbridge, *Beyond Adversary Democracy* (New York: Basic Books, 1980), esp. pts. II and IV.

49. Walzer, "Philosophy and Democracy," p. 391.

50. I explore the implications of this position for the case of health care in "For and Against Equal Access." See esp. pp. 555–58.

51. Walzer, "Philosophy and Democracy," p. 394.

52. For an answer based on constitutional interpretation that provides a critique of Ely's theory, see Walter F. Murphy, "An Ordering of Constitutional Values," *Southern California Law Review* 53, no. 2 (January 1980): 703–60; and Murphy, "Constitutional Interpretation: Text, Values, and Processes," *Reviews in American History*, March 1981, pp. 7–14.

53. In addition to Dworkin, see Frank I. Michelman, "Welfare Rights in a Constitutional Democracy," *Washington University Law Quarterly* 1979, no. 3 (Summer 1979): 659–93; Michelman, "In Pursuit of Constitutional Welfare Rights: One View of Rawls' Theory of Justice," *University of Pennsylvania Law Review* 121 (1973): 962–1019; Fiss, "The Forms of Justice," pp. 1–58; Bruce Ackerman, *Social Justice in the Liberal State* (New Haven: Yale University Press, 1980); and Tribe, *The Constitutional Protection of Individual Rights*. Not all of these constitutional theorists claim that all of the rights that they argue should be protected are protected by the existing Constitution.

54. For a more thoroughly argued consequentialist case for democracy, see William N. Nelson, *On Justifying Democracy* (London: Routledge & Kegan Paul, 1980).

55. See Dennis F. Thompson, *John Stuart Mill and Representative Government* (Princeton: Princeton University Press, 1976), pp. 36–53, 193–95. As Thompson indicates, this argument does not tell us how extensive the domain of democratic decisionmaking must be to achieve this effect.

56. Walzer, "Philosophy and Democracy," p. 392.

57. For an example of how little legislative deliberation and citizen participation it takes to pass a law protecting a substantial, and very costly, welfare interest, see Rettig's account of the passage in 1972 of Section 2991 of Public Law 92–603, which provided full government funding of renal dialysis, in "The Policy Debate," pp. 132–37.

58. Robert Dahl takes some important steps in this direction in an essay that came to my attention after writing this piece. See "The Moscow Discourse: Fundamental Rights in a Democratic Order," in *Government and Opposition* 15, no. 1 (Winter 1980): 3–30.

4

Taking Rights Frivolously

WALTER BERNS

I

We were asked to address the question of whether liberalism means anything today, which immediately raises the question of what we mean by liberalism. If we define it in contradistinction to conservatism, an approach to current political issues exemplified by, for example, President Reagan, liberalism means an approach to current political issues exemplified by, for example, Senator Tsongas. So defined, Senator Tsongas is evidently better qualified than I am to determine whether it means anything today. If, however, by liberalism we mean a political regime or, more simply, a politics that takes its bearings from, or that understands itself in terms of, or is founded on the rights of man, then, qualified or not, I shall hazard an answer to the question.

II

The United States was the first nation to found itself on liberal principles so understood. This happened, as Lincoln repeatedly reminded us, in 1776 when we not only declared our independence from Britain's George III but did so by appealing to "the Laws of Nature and of Nature's God" according to which all men are created equal insofar as they are endowed with the rights to life, liberty, and the pursuit of happiness. "[Liberal] governments are instituted among men [in order] to secure these rights, [and they derive] their just powers from the consent of the governed."

George III ruled by the Grace of God, and, nominally at least, so does his current successor, Elizabeth II. But according to the liberal principles of the Declaration of Independence, no one rules, not even the president, who merely "presides" over the public business; and those who govern do so only because the governed have given their consent. This follows from the fact that by nature all men are free in the respect that they are subject to no government except self-government. The Founders referred to this as a self-evident truth. However self-evident this was, in 1776 it was a newly discovered truth, and the United States, the first nation to be built on it, referred to itself as a *novus ordo seclorum,* a new order of the ages.

Thomas Hobbes can be credited with being liberalism's founding father. Regarding himself as the first political scientist, he discovered natural rights and deduced from them the laws of nature to which Jefferson and his colleagues referred in the Declaration. The rights men possess by nature cannot be secured in nature, or in the state of nature, because, Hobbes discovered, men are not social by nature; these rights could not be secured under the governments of his time because of the priests and lawyers—we would call them intellectuals—who exercised what Hobbes called "private judgment." They claimed the capacity to pronounce whether the laws were just or unjust. And, Hobbes asks, "how many rebellions hath this opinion been the cause of, which teacheth that the knowledge whether the commands of kings be just or unjust, belongs to private men, and that before they yield obedience, they not only may, but ought to dispute them?"[1] Because of this dangerous as well as, Hobbes insisted, unfounded opinion, life in the societies of the time, like life in the state of nature, resembled life under a state of war; and under a state of war, as we all have recited, the life of man is "solitary, poor, nasty, brutish, and short." Hobbes's solution to this problem took the form of an attempt to put moral and political philosophy, for the first time, on a scientific basis, so that the conclusions drawn from them would be indisputable. Political science would have the degree of authority attributed by all thinking men to Euclidean geometry. It would be based on self-evident truths. According to this new political science, in order to secure their rights men must give up their rights to a sovereign; security for rights required above all a government with powers.

John Locke, who used to be known as "America's philosopher" because he was so obviously the direct source of the Declaration of Independence, only apparently differed from Hobbes in this respect. "The great and chief end . . . of men's uniting into commonwealths and putting themselves under government is the preservation of their . . . lives, liberties, and estates, which I call by the general name 'property' . . . [T]o which in the state of nature there are many things wanting . . ." What was wanting or lacking in the state of nature were legislative, judicial, and executive powers.[2] To supply these defects, and thereby secure their rights, men agree to be governed by a sovereign—a sovereign of sorts—to whom or to which they yield the natural right by which they exercise these powers themselves.[3] Although he was not so forthright as Hobbes, especially in the places where he was in agreement with him, Locke, too, was persuaded that the alternative to a government with powers was likely to be war of everyone against everyone. "To avoid this state of war," Locke said, "is one great reason of men's putting themselves into society and quitting the state of nature . . ."[4] The state of nature has a law of nature to govern it, but, because of scarcity and the "corruption and viciousness of degenerate men,"[5] that law is not much obeyed. Hence, the powers men possess by natural right must be superseded by the political power they create when they contract with one another. To secure their rights, I repeat, men must first give up their rights.

Of course, they will do so under the impression that they will gain in the exchange, and both Hobbes and Locke promised them peace. In the same fashion, the Constitution promised "domestic tranquility," but Americans can now be excused for wondering whether the government has kept that promise. That it was *constitutionally* possessed with sufficient powers to keep its promises is the theme of Chief Justice Marshall's frequently quoted (and almost as frequently misunderstood) statement in *McCulloch* v. *Maryland.* The legislative powers, he wrote, are given in a Constitution "intended to endure for ages to come, and, consequently, [those powers are] to be adapted to the various crises of human affairs."[6] But the American government has not adapted its powers to deal effectively with the crisis brought about by the criminals who, especially in our cities, pose a real threat to our natural rights to life and liberty.

Hobbes was no less alert than Locke to the risks involved in this yielding of rights to civil society—what assurance did men have that the sovereign would not abuse the powers given him?—but he knew of no way in principle or in practice to guarantee that this would not happen. Locke agreed that, in principle, the sovereign must possess all the powers men possessed in the state of nature—which meant, whatever powers were needed to secure rights—but he discovered a way that, in practice, might provide the assurances men required. Whereas Hobbes's sovereign was the great Leviathan, Locke's was the legislative. The legislative is "the supreme power."[7] Political power is first of all the *"right of making laws* with penalties of death and, consequently, all less penalties for the regulating and preserving of property, and [secondly] of employing the force of the community in the execution of *such laws* and in the defense of the commonwealth from foreign injury. . . ."[8] The power that men have in the state of nature to do whatever is necessary to preserve themselves is given up "to be regulated *by laws* made by the society. . . ."[9]

The significance of this shift from Leviathan to legislative cannot be exaggerated; it represented the beginning of, or laid the foundation for, modern constitutionalism. In principle, laws can be as oppressive as the dictates of a Leviathan—in order to absolve themselves of blood guilt, for example, the Spartans annually passed a law in the form of a declaration of war that allowed them to kill their own Helots[10]—but laws are enacted by a legislature, and a legislature is limitable in practice. First, its members are aware that they, too, are subject to the laws they enact.[11] Second, by requiring that they be elected, the governed can hold legislators responsible. Third, there are institutional devices or arrangements that can serve to limit or at least moderate the powers of a legislature; for example, the legislative power can be distributed between two bodies and, as our veto provision demonstrates, even three bodies. In short, Locke made it possible to institutionalize sovereignty.

But it was the Hobbesian Pufendorf who first insisted that when men contract to form civil society they must specify the powers granted and the powers withheld.[12] So far as I have been able to determine, this was the beginning of the idea of a written constitution, which was destined to play so important a role in modern—and liberal—constitutionalism.[13] And it was Montesquieu—the "celebrated Montesquieu"[14]—who taught our Framers how to organize the powers they would specify in our written Constitution.

Much of what I have said to this point is encapsulated in *Federalist* 51. Madison writes:

> If men were angels, no government would be necessary [and if] angels were to govern men, neither external nor internal controls on government would be necessary. In framing a government which is to be administered by men over men [however], the great difficulty lies in this: you must first enable the government to control the governed; and in the next place oblige it to control itself. A dependence on the people is, no doubt, the primary control on the government; but experience has taught mankind the necessity of auxiliary precautions.[15]

The government instituted in 1787–88 in order to secure the rights of Americans is first of all a government of powers, powers by means of which the governed might be controlled, and, secondly, a government so organized that it will be obliged to control itself.

It is significant that in the original Constitution the word "right" appears only once, and then only in the context of Congress's power "to promote the progress of science and useful arts."[16] But, then, as Hamilton explained in *Federalist* 84, "the Constitution is itself, in every rational sense, and to every useful purpose, A BILL OF RIGHTS." It is a bill of natural rights, which it secures without mentioning them.[17]

III

Instead of specifying the rights of man after the fashion of the Declaration of Independence, the Constitution promises a more perfect union, justice, domestic tranquility, and provision for the common defense. In making these promises it is not unique; what makes it unique is the promise and the means by which it would fulfill the promise to "secure the blessings of liberty." Liberty can be denied by government, even democratic government, as well as by other men, and to guard against this eventuality was the principal task the Framers faced.

By liberty they meant the liberty to pursue private ends; indeed, as they understood it, liberalism is best characterized by liberty understood as privacy: the private economy, the private association, the private family, the private friendship, the private church or no-church, and all this with a view to a happiness privately defined. To secure this natural right above all, government is instituted among men.

Despite his reputation as a teacher of absolute government, it was Hobbes who first set down the principle by which liberal governments are guided. He argued that the first law of nature was to seek peace, and from this he deduced the second law of nature: *that a man be willing, when others are so too . . . to lay down their right to all things; and be contented with so much liberty against other men, as he would allow other men against himself.*[18] From these laws of nature Hobbes deduced his version of the Golden Rule, which is the principle on which liberalism rests: *"Do not that to another, which thou wouldest not have done to thyself."*[19] Not, as in the Biblical version, *do* unto others; Hobbes's rule was a deliberate reformulation of the Biblical version, for any *doing* unto others must of necessity reflect some notion of what is good or what ought to be done for or to others, and Hobbes understood all such notions to be merely vain opinions. Hence, in his reformulation, do *not* do unto others that which you do *not* want done to you. In brief, leave other men alone. Agree to leave other men alone in exchange for their promise to leave you alone, and agree to be governed by a sovereign who will enforce these promises.

Professor Mansfield's formulation allows us to understand how this might be accomplished:

> If men could stop disputing the ends of politics and agree on the condition of all ends, they could follow privately those ends whose pursuit is consistent with the same allowance to other ends. Under Hobbes's golden rule, the universe of tolerated ends is defined by the condition of all ends, including the intolerable, and that is civil peace. The end of government thus becomes security for those ends that can be represented.[20]

Men can in fact stop disputing the ends of politics—whether the regime should be a democracy, oligarchy, aristocracy, or monarchy, each promoting a way of life appropriate to its principle, or whether it should be a Christian (and, if so, what kind of Christian?), Jewish, or Fundamentalist Muslim commonwealth—if they can agree that governments are instituted not to promote one of these ends but rather to secure everybody's rights. A government organized to secure rights will represent us all in the sense that it will represent our rights. It will not represent our opinions, because these are likely to be opinions about ends and such opinions contradict one another. A government that attempts to represent opinions will become a House Divided and will not stand. At most, as Clifford Orwin has shown, it might represent opinions concerning "secondary and, strictly speaking, unpolitical matters."[21] In short, liberalism depends on representative government understood in this sense, and it was the American Framers' intention to establish such a government.

It can succeed only if there is general agreement among the opinion-holders that their opinions concern unpolitical matters. (There is no room in representative government for the Ayatollah Khomeini.) Which means that what were once understood to be ends must now be understood as matters of opinion on which men might differ. As Madison put it in *Federalist* 51, "In a free government the security for civil rights must be the same as that for religious rights. It consists in the one case in the multiplicity of interests, and in the other in the multiplicity of sects." Where there is a multiplicity of interests and sects, no one interest or sect is likely to be in a position to impose its rule on the others; or, no one of these interests will be in a position to transform itself from an interest to an end. Or, to state this in terms familiar to readers of *Federalist* 10, no "faction" will gain control of the government and impose its opinion of the end of government on others. Or, once more, and this time to refer back to Professor Mansfield's statement to the effect that the end of representative government is "security for those ends that can be represented," representative government represents ends transformed into interests. Such transformation makes it safe to represent them. Representative government is not government by Moral Majority. Under a properly structured representative government, Christianity and Judaism are seen as interests, not ends, and their advocates, instead of fighting religious wars, join ecumenical associations and speak of the "Judeo-Christian tradition." Live and let live is their motto.

IV

We do not much study representative government any more; we do not, in fact, study the Constitution. Courses in constitutional law are to be found in almost every law school and political science department, but there are very few courses on the Constitution, and none in the law schools. They teach future practitioners, some of whom will practice before the Supreme Court; the political science departments are likely to teach something they call judicial decisionmaking, which, as is well known, has little if anything to do with the Constitution. If they—law schools and political science departments—offer instruction in legal theory or jurisprudence, they are likely to do so out of Ronald Dworkin's influential book, *Taking Rights Seriously*, a book that takes the Constitution frivolously. Dworkin argues that rights—by which he does not mean rights as understood by the Framers of the Constitution—cannot be taken seriously until there has been a "fusion of constitutional law and moral theory." To make it clear that he is not referring to any moral theory that may have informed the Constitution as written, he finishes that sentence by saying that, in his judgment, that fusion "has yet to take place."[22] Be that as it may, when the law schools do not offer instruction in the Constitution, it is not wonderful (to use that word in its old sense) that the judges do not understand representative government.

In the course of holding unconstitutional the Georgia county unit system of counting votes, the Supreme Court, in an opinion written by Justice Douglas, said that the "conception of political equality from the Declaration of Independence, to Lincoln's Gettysburg Address, to the Fifteenth, Seventeenth, and Nineteenth Amendments can mean only one thing—one person, one vote."[23] This rule did not, however, dispose of the case because the issue in it had to do, not with the casting of votes, but with the counting or weighing of votes. As the Court said the following term, full and effective participation of all citizens in state government requires that "each citizen have an equally effective voice in the election of members of his state legislature." What the Court meant by "an equally effective voice" was made clear in the paragraph that followed: "Logically, in a society ostensibly grounded on representative government, it would seem reasonable that a majority of the people of a state could elect a majority of that state's legislators."[24] Votes were to be "weighed" in the legislature, presumably in terms of, or as units of, political influence. This became clearer in the recent cases dealing with the Voting Rights Act where the Court began to speak of vote "dilution," and defined "dilution" as the inability of a group of voters—so far, a group of nonwhite voters—to elect one of its own to the legislature.[25] In all this the Court was mistaken in its understanding of political equality and of the principles of representative government on which our society is "grounded."

According to the Declaration of Independence, precisely because all men *are* created equal, no man may rule another without his consent; hence, government may be instituted only with the consent of those who are to be governed. In the giving of this consent, every person has one vote and all votes are weighed equally. But this does not mean that the persons voting are forbidden to give their consent to a system of government in which votes will not be weighed equally, or, indeed, in which not everyone—for example, not children, not criminals, not the insane, not aliens—is permitted to vote. In other words, the majority is free to constitute a government in which the majority principle is modified. After all, government is instituted to "secure these [natural] rights," and it is altogether reasonable to assume that rights are not best secured under a government that is moved or actuated by simple majorities; such majorities may not respect the rights of minorities. Those who wrote and ratified the Constitution were not guided by Bentham's simple and insidious formula, the greatest good of the greatest number. A majority dedicated to achieving its greatest good is a majority that will transform its interest into an end; it will impose its rule on other interests, thereby depriving them of their right to be represented as interests. In Madison's language, such a majority is a faction. The chief task the Framers set for themselves was to guard "against such a faction, and at the same time to preserve the spirit and form of popular government."[26]

It was the Anti-Federalists, like the modern Supreme Court, that defined representation in terms of responsiveness to the electorate. Because the people cannot "present" themselves in the legislative assembly—their numbers and the great extent of territory preclude it—the Anti-Federalists called for an assembly in which the people would be re-presented; the legislative body would be a "mirror" or a "reflection" of the people. As Melancton Smith put it when speaking against the Constitution in the New York ratifying convention, the "idea that naturally suggests itself to our minds, when we speak of representatives, is, that they resemble those they represent." He then added that the collected representatives "should be a true picture of the people. . . ."[27]

According to the Framers, however, representation was a way of keeping the people out of government, or, in the emphatic words of *Federalist* 63, representation permitted *"the total exclusion of the people in their collective capacity"* from any share in the government. They saw no virtue in participation, to say nothing of participatory democracy. There was to be a distance between representative and represented, hence the electoral college, the original indirect election of Senators, longer terms of office, larger House districts (thereby encompassing "a greater variety of parties and interests," and thereby freeing members, more or less, from a dependence on any one group or "faction"). In all these ways, in addition to those structural devices such as bicameralism, separation of powers, and checks and balances, representative government will negate or minimize the influence of those opinions that cannot be safely represented. The country will be governed by constitutional majorities formed not in the society but in the legislative process. "[T]he society itself will be broken into so many parts, interests and classes of citizens, that the rights of individuals, or of the minority, will be in little danger from interested combinations of the majority."[28]

The Constitution was designed not only to negate or minimize the influence of those opinions that cannot safely be represented—let us call them intolerant opinions—but to reduce the number of persons holding such opinions. Here, too, the Framers were guided by Locke who, to speak metaphorically, was the founder of ecumenicalism.

He accomplished this by persuading men to devote their lives primarily to the acquisition of material goods, the means of comfortable preservation in this world, and only secondarily (if at all) to gaining salvation in another. The sermon from his mount can be stated as follows: lay up for yourselves treasures on earth (not in heaven), "for where your treasure is, there will your heart be also."[29] Locke made acquisitiveness respectable, and by so doing paved the way to capitalism and the bourgeois society. "The great and chief end," Locke said, "of men's uniting into commonwealths and putting themselves under government is the preservation of their property."[30] And by property narrowly understood he did not mean the possessions men manage to acquire in the state of nature—the berries, acorns, or the "little piece of yellow metal"[31]—but the property right, which is the right to acquire. It is to preserve this right that men put themselves under government. Madison was expressing Locke's view exactly when he said in *Federalist* 10 that "the protection of different and unequal faculties of acquiring property . . . is the first object of government."

The consequences flowing from this unleashing of the acquisitive passion will be a society hard at work and, as Locke predicted, a tremendous and continuing increase in the wealth of the nation. The Framers not only agreed with this but depended on it.[32] They depended on it because of the *political* consequences: free representative government will be possible. By protecting the equal *right* to acquire and the different and unequal *faculties* of acquiring, "the possession of different degrees and kinds of property immediately results," and from this ensues "a division of the society into different interests and parties."[33] Instead of being divided along sectarian, moral, or even class lines—that is, along the lines of intolerant opinions—American society will be comprised of a variety of economic interests, whose regulation, Madison then says, will form the principal task of modern legislation. With the great increase of wealth (and assuming its wide distribution), everybody will have more and will hope for still more, and the issues that will divide the society will be, compared to those dividing other societies, readily compromised in the legislative process. In a word, the *animosity* of factions will be replaced by the *competition* of interests. And interests, unlike moral opinions, or opinions about the end of government, are safely represented. The result will be a liberal society where men can live private lives. The Framers took the property right seriously because they took the right of privacy seriously.

V

Almost everyone seems to agree that American government is representative government—or, at least, that it ought to be representative government—but there is no agreement as to what or who should be represented, and there is now considerable disagreement as to the institutions through which this representation is to be accomplished. For example, there is a lively and continuing dispute concerning the role of the federal judiciary. Is it a representative institution, and, if so, what or whom does it represent?

Hamilton provided the original answer to these questions when, in *Federalist* 78, he said the judges have the duty to be "faithful guardians of the Constitution." As such, they represent the Constitution or, more precisely, the people of the United States from which it came. Unlike elected officials, especially members of the House of Representatives, the judges have no constituents, or, in the usual sense of that term, no living constituents.[34] In one respect at least, it can be said that the people they represent, or the people whose "will" is embodied in the Constitution, are no longer living.

On the other hand, the people now living have an interest in the perpetuation of the Constitution, and the judiciary can also be said to represent that interest, or that people in that respect. It might even be said that constitutionally we are the same people as we were in 1787, and that the Constitution is as much the product of our will as it was then; after all, "we the people" of 1787 acted for our "Posterity" as well as for ourselves. Thus, until we the people have, "by some solemn and authoritative act, annulled or changed the established form," said Hamilton, we are bound by it and the judges are bound to enforce it on us.[35] This means that the judiciary represents us, the people, but only in our sovereign or constituting capacity. The point to be stressed here is that, unlike elected officials who can be said to derive some (or, as some would have it, most) of their authority from their constituents, the judges derive their authority from the Constitution. "As representatives of the Constitution, judges may have to listen to representatives of the people, but it is not their office to represent the people, or to fancy themselves the interpreters or expositors of the will of living people [unless that will expresses itself in a constitutional change]; the Constitution provides other offices to do that."[36] The judiciary was not intended to be representative in the usual sense. As Henry Abraham has written, there is "not one shred of evidence in the debates of the Founding Fathers in the Constitutional Convention that there was *any* thought, let alone intention, on their part to provide a representative judiciary."[37]

Today, however, the argument is made that the judiciary might find it necessary to become representative when the other branches of government, federal as well as state and local, fail properly to represent. According to the friends of judicial activism, this happens on a regular basis if not all the time. Here, for example, is Abram Chayes on the subject: "And to retreat to the notion that the legislature itself—Congress!—is in some mystical way adequately representative of all the interests at stake, is to impose democratic theory by brute force on observed institutional behavior."[38]

Nothing is more popular in politics these days than criticism of Congress. This has reached the point where, in the words of Richard Fenno, wise candidates "run *for* Congress by running *against* Congress."[39] But, as Professor Chayes makes evident, Congress is sometimes (if not usually) criticized not for its failure to perform the functions assigned it by the Constitution, but for its failure to be democratic. Like the bureaucracy, the electoral college, and the political parties, Congress is accused of not being sufficiently responsive to popular opinion. In the extreme case, Jimmy Carter ran for the presidency by running against all of Washington, promising to make "the government as good as the people." It apparently never occurred to him that the Framers, because they had reason to doubt that the people themselves would be the best fiduciary of natural rights, intended to constitute a government better than the people. No doubt, the Congress is not beyond reproach, but before we replace representative government with government by judiciary (whose advocates—jurists and law professors—are more strategically placed than the advocates of popular government), it would be wise to examine their chief characteristics.

Representative government permits government by constitutional rather than simple majorities, majorities assembled not from among the people but, as I said earlier, from among their representatives. Americans have a constitutional right to be, through their representatives, a part of the process by which these majorities are assembled. They gained this constitutional right in exchange for their natural right to govern themselves. They do not have a constitutional right to have their opinions prevail, or a right to have their interests preferred over others. Since there will be a variety of interests represented, they have, at most, a right to have their interests weighed. Precisely because there will be a variety of interests, the constitutional majorities required for decision will have to be assembled, and there are rules governing this process, rules of behavior as well as of procedure. These rules encourage, and, indeed, require accommodation. For example, they require debate, which implies on the part of those participating in it a capacity and willingness to be persuaded. This means persuaded by another with an equal right to form a majority or to be a part of one, with an equally legitimate interest and, perhaps, with a superior argument. And it implies, even encourages, the willingness to abide by the vote of the majority assembled. The importance of this cannot be exaggerated. Those who participate in the process are not permitted to overlook, because the rules require them to recognize, the right of every representative to be part of a majority, or to overlook the fact that the purpose of forming majorities is to govern. Governing requires majorities. Free government especially is not a simple business, as representatives will come to realize as they seek the consent of those with different interests. This is calculated to affect the speeches they make. Representative government is characterized by speech whose purpose is to gain the consent of others, and the right to speak with a view to gaining consent is given constitutional protection in Article I.

To use the language of modern social science, this legislative process is not a zero-sum game. Its ability to avoid becoming a zero-sum game depends on its ability to exclude issues—the abortion issue comes to mind—on which there can be only one winner and one loser. This explains Madison's statement that the principal task of modern legislation will be the regulation of "various and interfering [property] interests."[40] And this is why American politics (on the *national* level) has, with a massive exception that proves the rule,* been dominated by or concerned to so great an extent with economic issues. It was supposed to be that way. As Mansfield points out, "[O]ne cannot defend one's own property without defending Property,"[41] or, perhaps, better, one cannot defend one's own right to acquire property without defending the right to acquire as such. To have a property interest, Mansfield goes on, "is to have a definite individual stake in a whole. It is to have a duty as well as a right." Contrary to Marx, and under a proper system of representative government, property interests can be accommodated, or, as Locke predicted, a society that secures the property right will be a peaceful society.

VI

We are told by a famous judge writing in a most prestigious law journal that the Warren Court especially should be praised for demonstrating to law students that there is "no theoretical gulf

---

*I am referring to the slavery issue and its vestiges.

between law and morality,"[42] which means, between the law of the Constitution and the judges' morality. In this statement may be glimpsed the relevant and salient difference between representative government and government by judiciary. For, whereas a properly structured legislature represents interests which it attempts to accommodate, the judiciary "represents" parties who claim to have rights, and it is rights that it dispenses. Not only does our judiciary dispense rights, it "creates" them—it creates constitutional rights[43]—and, to the extent that it does this, the language of rights becomes the language of our politics. That this has its problems has been acknowledged by James Q. Wilson:

> The language of rights now appears to be the governing jurisprudential theory of our law schools and law reviews and the dominant philosophy shaping citizen relations with the state and, increasingly, the corporation. That it is an inadequate philosophy can be readily shown, for it supplies no principles by which a conflict in individual rights can be settled and it leads to policies . . . that reduce the claims of some in order to advance the claims of others.[44]

When, for example, the Court makes a constitutional right of a woman's interest in not becoming a mother, there is no way it can accommodate the man's interest in becoming a father.[45] The judicial process is a zero-sum game.

Furthermore, these constitutional rights are fashioned out of moral claims—which is to say, the contemporary American judiciary is more accessible than is the Congress to moral claimants—and, as the Framers had reason to know, it is difficult and sometimes impossible to accommodate moral claims. They are frequently intolerant and, therefore, not safely represented in the legislature; they are no more safely represented in the judiciary.

For example, we have surely not seen the final consequences of *Roe* v. *Wade*.[46] The American public was, admittedly, not united on the ontological question underlying the abortion issue—What is being? Or when does it begin?—but it is now dangerously divided on it. The Court saw to that. Without any basis in the Constitution (which was wisely silent on the issue), the Court created a constitutional right, and, as a consequence, defined a battlefield on which single-moral-issue groups face each other like opposing armies. Thanks to the Court, the animosity of factions is replacing the competition of Madisonian interests in national politics. And at whose behest? Who brings these potentially divisive law suits?

Not the people. The constitutional right to privacy on which the Court relied in *Roe* v. *Wade* had its origins in the Connecticut birth control case (where Justice Douglas found it lurking in shadows cast by a potpourri of constitutional provisions[47]), but there was no compelling reason, political or constitutional, for the Court to assume jurisdiction in that case. The Constitution had nothing to say about birth control, and the political forces in Connecticut were so balanced that while one of them was strong enough to defeat any attempt to repeal the statute (which, of course, ought never to have been enacted), the other was strong enough to prevent it from being enforced. Only those who insist on a purity of principle—in this case, Yale professors—found it inconvenient to accept that situation. The people somehow manage to find representatives for their interests in the legislative process; they elect them. It is the so-called intellectuals, outvoted in the legislature, who go to court. They go to court because, as the courts are now constituted, they are more likely to win there.

This reminds us of Hobbes's complaint: the tendency of priests and lawyers to think they had a right to inject their "private judgments" into politics. Because such "intellectuals" posed the greatest threat to representative government, he began the process of thought that culminated in the arrangements by which their influence would be negated or at least minimized.

I close by quoting myself:

> It is as if the Court is of the opinion that taking rights seriously requires it to accord to demands or wants the status of rights, as if, by natural right, a person consents to be governed on the condition that his wants be satisfied. But this is absurd because it is impossible, and it is impossible because not all wants can be satisfied. (For example, the wants of the pro- and anti-abortion groups cannot both be satisfied.) What government can promise, if it is organized properly, is that rights can be secured, by which I mean the natural right to be governed only with one's consent. Under the Constitution's system of representative government, this becomes the right to be part of a governing majority.
>
> To repeat: while rights, properly understood, can be secured, not all wants can be satisfied. As our history attests, however, when those rights are secured, many wants are satisfied. Their satisfaction depends on their not being seen as rights.[48]

Notes

1. Hobbes, *De Cive*, Preface to the Reader.
2. Locke, *Treatises*, II, secs. 124, 125, 126.
3. Ibid., secs. 129, 130.
4. Ibid., sec. 21.
5. Ibid.; sec. 128.
6. *McCulloch* v. *Maryland*, 4 Wheaton, 316, 415 (1819). Despite the frequent statements to the contrary, Marshall's meaning is not that the Constitution is adaptable—its meaning is fixed. He means the powers must be adaptable, which is clear from the statement that immediately follows in his opinion. This is put beyond any doubt in an essay he published in the *Alexandria Gazette* in which, with specific reference to his *McCulloch* statement concerning adaptation, Marshall says that its "sole object is to remind us that a constitution cannot possibly enumerate the means by which

the powers of government are to be carried into execution." See Gerald Gunther, ed., *John Marshall's Defense of McCulloch v. Maryland* (Stanford: Stanford University Press, 1969), p. 185.

7. Locke, *Treatises*, II, sec. 131.

8. Ibid., sec. 3. Emphasis supplied.

9. Ibid., sec. 131. Emphasis supplied.

10. Plutarch, "Lycurgus."

11. Locke, *Treatises*, II, sec 93.

12. Pufendorf, *Of the Law of Nature and Nations*, trans. by Oldfather & Oldfather (Oxford: Clarendon Press, 1934), bk. II, ch. 3, #13–15 (pp. 202–8); bk. VII, ch. 2, #6, 7, 8 (pp. 974–77); bk. VII, ch. 6, #2, 3 (pp. 1055–56); bk. VII, ch. 6, #9 (p. 1066). See also Walter Berns, "Judicial Review and the Rights and Laws of Nature," in *The Supreme Court Review—1982*, edited by Philip B. Kurland (Chicago: The University of Chicago Press, 1983), pp. 49–83.

13. Of the 164 countries in the world, all but 7 (among them the United Kingdom, New Zealand, and Israel) have written constitutions.

14. *Federalist* 47, 78.

15. *Federalist* 51.

16. Art. I, sec. 8, #8.

17. See Walter Berns, "The Constitution as Bill of Rights," in *How Does the Constitution Secure Rights?*, edited by Robert A. Goldwin and William A. Schambra (Washington, D.C.: American Enterprise Institute, 1982).

18. Hobbes, *Leviathan*, ch. 14.

19. Ibid., ch. 15.

20. Harvey C. Mansfield, Jr., "Hobbes and the Science of Indirect Government," *The American Political Science Review* 65 (March 1971): 107.

21. Clifford Orwin, "Representative Government and Its Discontents," pp. 24–25. Unpublished paper.

22. Ronald Dworkin, *Taking Rights Seriously* (Cambridge: Harvard University Press, 1977), p. 149.

23. *Gray v. Sanders*, 372 U.S. 368, 381 (1963).

24. *Reynolds v. Sims*, 377 U.S. 533, 565 (1964).

25. See, for example, *United Jewish Organizations v. Carey*, 430 U.S. 144, 162 (1977).

26. *Federalist* 10.

27. Jonathan Elliot, *The Debates in the Several State Conventions on the Adoption of the Federal Constitution* (Philadelphia: Lippincott, 1888), vol. 2, p. 245.

28. *Federalist* 51.

29. Matthew 6:19–21.

30. Locke, *Treatises*, II, sec. 124.

31. Ibid., sec. 37.

32. Here is *Federalist* 12 on this subject: "The prosperity of commerce is now perceived and acknowledged by all enlightened statesmen to be the most useful as well as the most productive source of national wealth, and has accordingly become a primary object of their political cares. By multiplying the means of gratification, by promoting the introduction and circulation of the precious metals, those darling objects of human avarice and enterprise, it serves to vivify and invigorate all the channels of industry and to make them flow with greater activity and copiousness. The assiduous merchant, the laborious husbandman, the active mechanic, and the industrious man-ufacturer—all orders of men look forward with eager expectation and growing alacrity to this pleasing reward of their toils."

33. *Federalist* 10.

34. Walter Berns, "The Least Dangerous Branch, But Only If . . . ," in *The Judiciary in a Democratic Society*, edited by Leonard J. Theberge (Lexington, Mass.: Lexington Books, 1979), p. 12.

35. *Federalist* 78.

36. Berns, "The Least Dangerous Branch," p. 12.

37. Henry J. Abraham, "Reflections on the Recruitment, Nomination, and Confirmation Process to the Federal Bench," p. 23. A paper prepared for a conference on the federal courts, Washington, D.C., American Enterprise Institute, October 1980.

38. Abram Chayes, "The Role of the Judge in Public Law Litigation," *Harvard Law Review* 89 (May 1976): 1311.

39. Richard F. Fenno, Jr., "U.S. House Members in Their Constituencies: An Exploration," *The American Political Science Review* 71 (September 1977): 914.

40. *Federalist* 10.

41. Harvey C. Mansfield, Jr., *The Spirit of Liberalism* (Cambridge: Harvard University Press, 1978), p. 93.

42. J. Skelly Wright, "Professor Bickel, the Scholarly Tradition, and the Supreme Court," *Harvard Law Review* 84 (February 1971): 804.

43. It was in the course of dissenting from a creative judgment that Justice White said that although "the Court has ample precedent for the creation of new constitutional rights [that] should not lead it to repeat the process at will." *Moore* v. *City of East Cleveland*, 431 U.S. 494, 544 (1977).

44. James Q. Wilson, "What Can Be Done?" *AEI 1980 Public Policy Week Papers* (Washington, D.C.: The American Enterprise Institute, 1980), p. 10.

45. *Planned Parenthood of Central Missouri* v. *Danforth*, 428 U.S. 52 (1976).

46. *Roe* v. *Wade*, 410 U.S. 113 (1973).

47. *Griswold* v. *Connecticut*, 381 U.S. 479, 484 (1965).

48. Berns, "The Constitution as Bill of Rights."

5

Toward a Liberal Foreign Policy

MARSHALL COHEN

Liberalism is, among other things, the political manifestation of a distinctive moral philosophy. According to this philosophy political institutions and public arrangements should acknowledge and respect the moral equality of individuals.[1] In our society liberals are inclined to think this requires guaranteeing certain fundamental rights and liberties, including the right to political participation, and they are also likely to think it requires a more egalitarian distribution of material resources than we have so far achieved. Liberals generally believe that we have a moral obligation to support the realization of these principles not only in our own society but in other societies as well. Needless to say, there are many who dissent from some, or even from all, of these views, and on a variety of grounds.

In this essay I shall be describing a certain type of dissent from liberal policies that is often described as conservative, and I shall be considering some of the doctrines on which this sort of dissent relies. But it is worth saying at once that there are many different types of conservatives—religious authoritarians, Burkeans, libertarians, and moral populists to mention only a few—and many subtle blendings of what I am calling liberal and conservative opinion as well. I shall be content if the reader finds in this typology a rough approximation to constellations and tendencies of opinion that manifest themselves on the contemporary American scene. I am not concerned, however, to defend the historical legitimacy of this usage of the terms "liberal" and "conservative" or to deny that there is a larger sense of the term "liberal" in which the main body of American opinion is in a sound and significant sense liberal.

I am grateful to Michael Doyle, Amy Gutmann, Nathan Tarcov, and especially to Thomas Scanlon for helpful remarks about earlier versions of this essay.

Some of those who reject liberal attitudes about international affairs do so because they reject the liberal's belief in the moral equality of all people. I shall not discuss this point of view here because, although it is undoubtedly held by many Americans, it is not very often openly held or frankly defended. Arguments appealing to this view are not respectable in American public discourse and so far as I am concerned that is all to the good. Others who reject liberal attitudes do so because they think that moral considerations are simply irrelevant to the conduct of foreign affairs. This is a very influential view and I shall consider it shortly. First, however, I wish to call attention to the position of those who reject liberal attitudes while sharing the liberal's commitment to morality and even to moral equality. These critics of liberalism simply differ from liberals in their understanding of what moral equality requires.[2] They often argue that while moral equality requires the recognition of a few fundamental rights it does not require the expansive list of rights liberals propose. They sometimes claim, for instance, that moral equality requires the enjoyment of "negative" but not of "positive" liberties.[3] They may agree, then, that men possess a right to personal security and even to certain personal freedoms, but they may regard the denial of a right to political participation as fully compatible with the requirements morality places on the structure of political institutions. The conservative's attitude toward the moral legitimacy of undemocratic governments will therefore differ sharply from the liberal's.

Again, many conservatives who accept the principle of moral equality reject the liberal view that implementing it requires a more egalitarian distribution of material resources. Liberals think that greater equality of distribution is necessary to give substance to the right of political participation and to provide men with a fair chance of achieving a measure of dignity and personal autonomy. Only in this way can men develop their own talents and faculties (including their moral faculties) and in some degree determine their own fates. For this reason liberals do not accept the view that the uncorrected allocations of the international market (since they result from exercising the right to contract) satisfy the requirements of moral equality. They will certainly reject the libertarian suggestion that any attempt to make such corrections constitutes an affront to the moral dignity and fundamental rights of those who presently possess unreasonable shares. It is, then, in their attitude to the propriety of undemocratic regimes and to the acceptability of the present international economic order that the moral positions of liberals and conservatives most clearly diverge.

Some will think this contrast overdrawn for, as they see it, liberals as well as conservatives support undemocratic regimes—liberals because the suppression of democratic rights is sometimes necessary for economic progress, conservatives because authoritarianism is often the only alternative to totalitarianism. There are, as I have suggested, many kinds of liberals and many kinds of conservatives. I do not wish to deny that some who very reasonably call themselves conservatives have a commitment to democratic rights that is as sincere as the liberal's or that like liberals they accept undemocratic governments only *faute de mieux* and with a deep sense of regret. In my opinion, however, liberals and conservatives often accept such claims of "necessity" far too uncritically, and I would contend that no true liberal could regard the suppression of political rights for those who desire them, and who could reasonably exercise them, as anything but a serious violation of moral rights, which it is important to overcome. (It goes without saying that Marxists and other leftists who have contempt for "bourgeois" rights are not liberals in my sense.)

By contrast, many conservatives do not share this moral view of the fundamental nature of the right to political participation, and some unquestionably have more than a little sympathy for the undemocratic and authoritarian governments they find it "necessary" to support. Indeed, this hostility to democratic government sometimes manifests itself even at home. Many conservatives think that the democratic masses should be excluded from the fine art of establishing foreign policies, where their ignorance and untamed democratic ardors often interfere with the true statesman's rather different agenda.

I have so far described as conservative those who accept the ideal of moral equality, although they interpret it differently from liberals. There is another moral difference worth noticing, however. Many conservatives, in addition to rejecting the liberal's strong interpretation of the ideal of moral equality, also reject the liberal's claim that we have a weighty obligation to help others implement the requirements of moral equality. Indeed, some conservatives think our obligation to others is so weak that we are even permitted to achieve our own purposes at their expense and by denying them the elementary rights and basic resources we already possess. Thus, even some of the democratically inclined conservatives I mentioned above are prepared to sacrifice the democratic liberties and frustrate the economic aspirations of others if doing so will marginally increase our own security or advance the economic interests of our own nation. Conservatives of this sort often regard the universalistic tendencies of liberalism as sentimental or even utopian. By contrast, the liberal is inclined to regard them as requirements internal to the notion of morality itself.

The conservatives we have so far considered do not contest the liberal's claim that our foreign relations must be founded on moral principles. They simply disagree, although sometimes very sharply, about what morality actually requires. From a theoretical point of view, then, a still more fundamental challenge to the liberal point of view is presented by those skeptics and realists who deny that morality possesses any authority in the realm of international affairs. In their view the pursuit of the national interest provides the only legitimate guide to conduct in what is an autonomously political realm. In George Kennan's words, it is a realm not "fit" for moral judgment. Of course, the political calculations of those who take the realist approach sometimes issue in policies that coincide with those the liberal endorses. The realist may think our nation is safer in a more democratic world or that our long-run prospects for a tranquil existence are better if others live decent lives and are not tempted to lay their misery and misfortune at our door. But from a liberal point of view this kind of reasoning (sound as it sometimes is) does not place liberal policies on a proper moral foundation, and it is frequently used to support policies that are offensive from a liberal point of view. All too often the national interest is identified with an uninhibited pursuit of national security and of national economic advantages if, in fact, the two are distinguished.

From a theoretical point of view there is an important difference between the moralist who assigns his obligation to his own countrymen a differential, and very heavy, weight and the realist who refuses to consider moral issues at all. But from a practical point of view the conservative moralist and the skeptical realist often subscribe to the same policies, and these are policies that violate liberal principles. It is, of course, often difficult to tell what the theoretical foundations of a particular conservative's views are. But it is permissible to suspect that many conservatives who employ moral language are in fact moral skeptics, and especially so about international affairs. We may not believe that Hobbes and the realists are correct in thinking that in the international realm moral language can only be used ideo-logically and strategically, but there is little doubt that it often is so used, and many who avail themselves of moral language are certainly indifferent to moral considerations or actively skeptical about their pertinence to international affairs. Moral skepticism of this sort constitutes the profoundest and, among those who are often entrusted with the conduct of foreign affairs, perhaps the most influential threat to a liberal philosophy of international relations. A critical examination of this point of view is, therefore, the first task of a liberal philosophy of foreign affairs.

Writers who are skeptical about a moral assessment of international affairs often possess a wholly inadequate conception of the require-ments of morality. At their most naive they identify moral conduct with conformity to rules, often to very simple, exceptionless rules like those forbidding lying or killing. When they discover that lying and killing are sometimes legitimate or justifiable in international affairs they conclude that legitimacy in this realm must be judged by nonmoral, or political, criteria. They fail to understand that moral rules may have exceptions, that moral requirements may be relative to circumstances and, even when they do not make these mistakes, that moral requirements may come into conflict. They understand well enough that in private life moral rules may come into conflict and that the right thing to do, what morality requires in these cases, is that we act on the weightier obligation. But if a nation violates a legal obligation in order to prevent a war, theorists of this sort do not offer a comparable analysis. Typically, they say that the nation acted not on ethical but on political grounds, and in acknowledging that it acted as it should they think we acknowledge the propriety of political rather than of ethical standards in the international realm. Of course, the nation may have acted on political rather than on ethical grounds. But this will have to be shown, and often it will not be possible to show anything more untoward or alarming than that in a situation in which the nation had to choose between moral obligations it chose the more compelling one. It does not follow from the fact that the realm of international politics often presents very difficult, and even tragic, choices that it is a realm in which it is impossible to tell, or to do, right or wrong. Realists often allege that only the political naïveté of moralists permits them to suppose this. Moralists may reply, however, that the real problem is to be located in the philosophical naïveté of the realists' ethical theory.

It would be foolish to deny that liberals have themselves often held similarly naive views of the nature of morality. Instead of meeting the problem by concluding that international affairs is exempt from morality, liberals of this sort have denounced international conduct and insisted that it be judged by what they take to be the only acceptable standards. R. B. Mowat, for instance, deplores the morality of princes because, in his view, "There can be no moral law which is categorical and not categorical at the same time; it cannot bind the individual and not bind the state. The Ten Commandments and the Golden Rule are universal propositions, without reservations, without exceptions."[4] And it is possible, though by no means certain, that (as Hans Morgenthau suggests) Woodrow Wilson was making a similar mistake when he said to Congress on declaring war in 1917 that he sensed "the beginning of an age in which it will be insisted that the same standards of conduct and responsibility for wrong shall be observed among nations and their governments that are observed among the individual citizens of civilized states."[5] However that may be, liberalism is not committed to such simplicities, and there will be more than enough to deplore in the realm of international affairs even when the complexities of moral judgment and the special circumstances of international affairs are taken into account.

A second tradition of skepticism is animated less by the inability to reconcile its notions of legitimate political conduct with its conception of decent moral conduct than it is by its view of politics as essentially the pursuit of power. Theorists of this sort often speak of the realm of politics as an autonomous and amoral realm, and in doing so they create a problem for themselves when they go on to draw a sharp distinction between domestic and international politics. They often insist that it is in the international realm that "power politics" holds sway, and they regard the failure to appreciate the fundamental differences between domestic and international politics as a characteristic and fatal error of liberals like Wilson who hope to overcome power politics and "balance of power" strategies as the governing principles of international politics. There is, of course, a great deal to be said for the realist's view that there are immensely important differences between the two realms, differences that some classical liberals have obscured. Nevertheless, if the essence of politics can be tempered in the domestic realm in a way that makes ethical conduct possible, it is legitimate to wonder why the essentialist argument that politics is a struggle for power should be thought so decisive in the international realm.

Realists who maintain that international politics is power politics generally claim that a statesman must take the national interest to be his "one guiding star, one standard of thought, one rule for action."[6] From the liberal moralist's point of view this doctrine is plainly unacceptable for it suggests that if it is in the national interest to violate the territorial integrity or political independence of another people, not to mention more Thucydidean or even Hitlerian possibilities, this is permitted or perhaps even required. (It is unclear in most realist writings whether the statesman is instructed to do whatever it is in the national interest to do or, more weakly, simply to do nothing that it is not in the national interest to do.) Of course, it may be that long-run prudence suggests upholding the established structure of the international system by abjuring actions of this sort, and it may even be that because its citizens would deplore such actions it will not be in the national interest to perform them. (Indeed, liberals are inclined to press against practitioners of power politics the fact that democratic citizens are unlikely to support pure power politics and, also, that the arts of secret diplomacy and of managing the "balance" are, in fact, incompatible with domestic moral and political requirements.) But in the end it will not be satisfactory to the liberal moralist to have liberal policies founded on morally neutral requirements of the national interest; as we have seen, to accept this doctrine is to accept the legitimacy of whatever the national interest turns out to be.

The transition from the inevitability of power politics to the desirability of a balance of power policy is often made with unpersuasive rapidity. And it is in fact not clear that pursuing a balance policy will inevitably further the national interest, for such a policy (whose ultimate justification may be to achieve certain international objectives, e.g., to prevent the hegemony of a single state) requires a certain restraint and insists on conformity to a desirable distribution or pattern of power that it may not be in the interest of the strong, or of the ideologically committed, to observe. But if pursuing a balance is not necessarily equivalent to pursuing the national interest, it is equally offensive to liberal principles and to the liberal sensibility and it has been the object of liberal criticism from Cobden to Wilson to the present, for if the balance requires the partition of Poland, the colonization of Africa, or the destabilization of Chile, these actions will have to be taken.

Then, too, the balance principle implies that alliances must not be formed on a moral or principled basis. Francis I may have shocked Europe when he allied with the Turks against Charles V, but he was acting on balance of power principles that set the proper standard in the eyes of realist commentators.[7] Therefore, for theorists of this sort a liberal alliance, dedicated to furthering the liberal interest and to expanding a Kantian zone of peace among republican states, could never be justified if it disturbed such a balance. It is on some such principles as these that balance of power or "sphere of influence" thinkers like George Kennan suggest that the Russian hegemony over Poland must be accepted today. But while liberal politics must scrutinize constellations of power and act only after a prudent assessment of risks and consequences, it cannot confine international political objectives to amoral manipulations and settlements of power. Liberal politics aims to advance the reach of liberal principles, and it willingly makes sacrifices to do so. These sacrifices will have to include risking the securities of the status quo balance of power. Liberals have never sided with Metternichs or Kissingers, and they are not entirely comfortable with Kennans, either.

Of course, nations cannot ordinarily be expected to sacrifice their very existence. It is for this reason that national interest and balance of power theories are most plausible or, as I think, only plausible, when they are combined with the assumption that nations exist in a state of nature. This is the third of the sources of moral skepticism that we must examine. It has been maintained by theorists from Hobbes to Raymond Aron that nations exist in a state of nature and that in a state of nature (as Hobbes says) there can be neither justice nor injustice. If all one can do in international politics is to maintain one's very existence there will be little room (except perhaps in observing *jus in bello*) for pursuing a liberal foreign policy.

I will not here contest Hobbes's view that there is neither justice nor injustice in the state of nature because it lacks a sovereign whose commands establish right and wrong. This view reflects a kind of ethical skepticism, or law-based ethics, that is unacceptable in any form. Nor will I press the argument that since this view concedes to individuals and nations a right of self-preservation it has thereby admitted by implication that the concepts of justice and injustice apply in the state of nature. Rather, I will deny (as Hobbes himself conceded) that states are as vulnerable as individuals in the state of nature. Certainly, it is not true that in the Hobbesian sense they are equal: it is not true that the weakest (state) can kill the strongest. Self-defense is not always the exclusive, or the overriding, objective of national policy.

The nineteenth-century United States, for instance, because of its size, its location, and the protection of the British navy, enjoyed a high degree of security.[8] Large, well-armed nations and nations protected by oceans and mountain ranges are often in a similarly secure situation and do not live in a condition of Hobbesian fear. They are in a position to show restraint, to calm the fears of others, and even to create the conditions of peace. Often it is their duty to do so. It is also important to notice that, in contrast to Hobbesian individuals, nations can often improve their security in ways that need not alarm others. Their best defense is not always an attack, and they can often give evidence of their peaceful intentions by choosing weapons and strategies that do not threaten others. They can build forts, mount fixed guns, mine harbors or, like the Russians, build wide-gauge railway tracks that are useless to invaders. They can also train civilian militias, study guerrilla warfare, and prepare themselves for passive resistance.

To be sure, there are circumstances in which these defensive choices could be aspects of a fundamentally aggressive design, but this is not invariably the case and it will not always seem to be the case. Individuals in the Hobbesian state of nature are anonymous and ahistorical. But nations have names and reputations, geographies and histories, principles and purposes, and these allow others to judge their intentions with considerable confidence. Sometimes these intentions will in fact be cooperative and even friendly, for nations have allies, belong to regional blocs, engage in mutually beneficial trade, and support larger cultural enterprises. They will often have strong moral reasons to perpetuate these relationships. Hobbes's suggestion that because nations retain their sovereign independence they must be in a state of war in which every nation has a "known disposition" to attack every other and in which no "assurance" can be obtained flies in the face of the evidence and suggests the presence of a stubborn philosophical thesis that its proponents are unwilling or unable to submit to empirical test.

Some have argued that the advent of nuclear weapons brings the international realm closer to the Hobbesian state of nature than it has ever been before. As David Gauthier observes, "Each new effort we undertake to increase our security merely increases the insecurity of others, and this leads them to new efforts which reciprocally increase our own insecurity. This is the natural history of the arms race—a history which bids fair to conclude, later if not sooner, in mutual annihilation."[9] But some of the observations we have made about the prenuclear period are relevant to the nuclear era as well, and they show that while we may in fact get ourselves into the situation Gauthier describes, that is by no means inevitably the case even in the absence of a world sovereign.

The Hobbesian situation is most closely approximated when both sides rely on vulnerable weapons that are capable of destroying weapons on the other side (highly accurate missiles in unhardened silos).[10] As in the classic Western gun duel the obvious strategy in such circumstances is to "anticipate," to shoot and shoot first. The nation that shoots first can hope to ensure its own safety by destroying its opponent's nuclear arsenal, and if it has enough left over, it can destroy the opponent's entire population as well. But if it delays the reluctant nation may suffer the same fate itself. Of course, if a first strike should fail, a nuclear response would probably be forthcoming, and whether this was initially a counterforce strike against silos and other military targets (of the sort that many war-fighting theorists propose) or a countercity strike against civilian populations (as some of the classical deterrence theorists imagine), the chances are considerable that (possibly after some escalation) the side initiating the exchange, and very likely that both sides, would be destroyed utterly.

Nevertheless, the existence of nuclear weapons does not make a situation of this sort inevitable. By confining themselves to second-strike weapons nuclear powers can make it clear that they do not intend to initiate nuclear war. If both sides acquire invulnerable, second-strike weapons neither side can, by striking first, destroy the other side's deterrent, its capacity to strike back. If a nuclear nation strikes, it must be prepared to pay the penalty. In this situation there is far less reason to jump the gun and less reason to fear that others will do so.

It is not true that in the nuclear world "each new effort we take to increase our security merely increases the insecurity of others, and . . . leads them to new efforts which reciprocally increase our own insecurity." We can increase our second-strike capability without increasing the insecurity of others. And to the extent that they are likely to strike in fear of losing their deterrent, we can, as Oscar Morgenstern suggested, increase our own security by helping our adversaries make their own second-strike forces invulnerable. Their insecurity increases our insecurity, and we can therefore increase our security by increasing theirs. The fact that nuclear nations can destroy one another's populations unquestionably strengthens the analogy between the individual and the international state of nature. But the fact that (unlike Hobbesian men or gun duellers) nuclear nations with adequate and secure second-strike forces can count on responding after they have been hit undermines it. The balance created by the equality of Hobbesian men, or by the "equalizer" of the Old West, is unstable, but the nuclear balance is capable of stability if one nation cannot, by "anticipating," prevent the other from making a devastating reply.[11] In these circumstances there may be no advantage in striking first and, if they are prudent, nuclear nations will see that it is irrationally risky to strike at all.

The fundamental moral obligation of the nuclear age is to avoid nuclear war. In anything like contemporary conditions this implies a strong obligation to renounce a first use of nuclear weapons, whether tactical or strategic. It is essential to maintain a rigorous distinction between conventional and nuclear war, and even those who deny that the only legitimate function of nuclear weapons is to deter the use of nuclear weapons should agree that their only other legitimate function is to respond to their use. Certainly nuclear weapons should not be used to compensate (if indeed they can compensate) for the inadequate provision of conventional forces. Buying more bang for the buck in this domain is, truly, a kind of bargaining with the devil. More generally, it is essential to maintain the nuclear balance. This stability will, of course, be lost if either side believes that the adequacy and invulnerability of its retaliatory weapons is endangered and that it must either use them or lose them. There is a strong obligation, therefore, to eschew the development of a first-strike capability that threatens the security of an adversary's deterrent if reciprocal restraint can be obtained. In appropriate circumstances, then, it will be morally inexcusable to reject measures (like arms control agreements with adequate inspection schemes) that will reassure one's opponent or to develop alarming numbers of weapons whose capabilities are ambiguous on the theory that their purpose is deterrent. These are precisely the weapons that can return us to a Hobbesian dilemma in which what one side believes, or claims to believe, are defensive or, in this case, deterrent weapons look to the other side like offensive, first-strike weapons.

It is especially important in situations of serious conflict to try to see ourselves as others see us. This is always a weighty consideration for those in Hobbesian situations.[12] But it is a supremely weighty one in the nuclear situation where the acquisition of ambiguous weapons (or of unambiguous ones in threatening numbers) can easily be misinterpreted by others with disastrous effects. Moral blindness in this area may bind us all to the final wheel of fire. The Hobbesians could not be more wrong. It is precisely in what they regard as a state of nature that men and nations must acknowledge their most awesome moral responsibilities.

There is, then, no possibility of escaping moral decisions even if nations are in the state of nature. But even if some aspects of international reality are usefully viewed as taking place in a state of nature, because self-defense is the overriding problem or because reliable expectations of mutual conformity to laws and conventions cannot be expected, this is by no means universally the case. Once outside the state of nature it is all the clearer that conduct cannot be governed (as much conservative thought supposes) simply by appeal to the national interest or to the requirements of the balance of power.

At this point, however, it will be useful to consider some of the major problems that confront American foreign policy and to observe the characteristically different ways in which liberals and conservatives approach them. We have emphasized the fact that liberals are committed to distinctive moral ideas and these ideas will often inform their approach to foreign policy. But liberalism as we know it is more than a particular philosophy; it is a complex tradition of thought and the expression of a distinctive sensibility as well. Liberals emphasize the potentialities of human reason and the common interests of men. They characteristically make a greater effort to see themselves as others see them and to assess the legitimacy of American policies from a disinterested point of view. They are more inclined than conservatives to seek political accommodations and to be more suspicious of military confrontations and solutions. They frequently have greater faith in the intrinsic appeal of human liberty and are therefore more willing to take their chances on its ultimate vindication if mankind survives in circumstances that are favorable to progress and justice. Speaking of the possibility of perpetual peace in his *Philosophy of Law* (the prospect of peace under law is a persistent liberal theme), Kant, perhaps the greatest of liberal thinkers, says that "although the realization of this purpose may always remain but a pious wish, yet we do certainly not deceive ourselves in adopting the maxim of action that will guide us in working incessantly for it; for it is a duty to do this."[13]

The governing objective of a liberal foreign policy must be to protect not all the interests, but the distinctively liberal interests of the United States and its liberal allies. A secondary objective will be to liberalize the Soviet world and ultimately the Soviet Union itself, which is not simply the main adversary of the United States, but a state opposed in principle to the liberal conception of society and a profound threat to liberal nations. The liberal's attitude is generally one of tolerance, but there is no avoiding the fact that from a liberal perspective these regimes can only be viewed as morally illegitimate. It is, however, a stubborn fact that liberal objectives cannot be advanced in a world that is overwhelmed by a nuclear catastrophe. The immediate aim of a liberal policy must be, then, to avoid nuclear war while protecting the liberal world.

In general, liberals believe that in present circumstances we should seek a situation of stable deterrence and supplement it with a no-first-use policy.[14] From a liberal point of view the willingness of conservatives (and of much European opinion) to contemplate the use of nuclear weapons in response to conventional aggression suggests a failure to imagine fully, and to evaluate soberly, the consequences not only for liberal values but for any civilized values that a policy of this sort risks. Most liberals do not despair of our ability to mount an adequate conventional defense and they think, in any case, that a liberal civilization is more likely to reemerge after a Soviet victory than it is after a nuclear holocaust. They prefer a future of insurrection to one of incineration.

If the conservative differs from the liberal in his willingness to deter conventional war with nuclear threats, he also differs from the liberal in his readiness to "deter" a Soviet attack with counterforce weapons that can only be viewed as provocative and destabilizing by the Soviets. It seems so clear to the liberal that this approach increases, rather than decreases, the likelihood of nuclear war that the liberal is inclined to believe that those who support it are pursuing objectives beyond simple deterrence. Some of these "flexible response" theorists undoubtedly think an arms race will undermine the Soviet economy. Others feel that because we have the technical and economic resources to achieve "escalation dominance" at every level, the world's perception of our superiority will increase our political prestige and allow us a broader range of military options at lower military levels.

Then, too, there are those who believe deterrence will ultimately fail. In their view Soviet leaders think they can defeat the United States in a nuclear war for which the Soviets are even now preparing. (Most liberals are more doubtful that Soviet leaders are willing to risk the consequences this course of action might impose on their own society.) In any case, it is not surprising that conservative strategists who interpret Soviet thinking in this way believe we ourselves could "prevail" in a sustained nuclear exchange. Indeed, some of them believe that targeting the Soviet leadership could lead to the collapse of the Soviet state and to the liberation of Soviet society.[15] Although fighting this winnable war is generally presented as something we would do reluctantly, and only after deterrence failed, it is pardonable to suspect (as surely the Soviets suspect) that strategists who think nuclear war likely or even inevitable also think it rational that we should strike first. It must certainly have occurred to them that we could try to put the Soviets in precisely the position they think the Soviets are trying to put us.

No doubt, some of the differences between liberals and conservatives are simply differences of opinion about what will in fact deter nuclear war. But in much of what they hear on the American right, liberals discern an insufficient willingness to seek mutual security, a refusal to see how our actions look to others, a reckless courting of unimaginable violence in the vain hope of political advantage, and a demonization of the Communist adversary that is implausible and ultimately self-defeating. These are not simply technical differences. They are differences of philosophy and of attitude.

It is not only in the nuclear area that the liberal finds many assessments of Soviet capacities and intentions implausible. This is a general feature of much American conservative thought, and in the liberal's opinion the American right often exaggerates the extent to which our foreign policy problems are caused by the Soviets. It follows that liberals are often skeptical of the view that opposing the Soviets is the way to resolve them. The rise of OPEC and the fall of the Shah (two major recent setbacks for American policy) were not Soviet-inspired, and the problems of the Caribbean have more to do with indigenous discontents and historic American policies than they do with present Soviet (or even Cuban) policies and actions.

Similarly, forming and arming an anti-Soviet coalition in the Middle East is far less important than settling the Arab-Israeli feud. These opponents fear each other more than they fear the Soviets, and their enmity constitutes a more imminent threat to our Middle Eastern interests than a Soviet invasion does. In any case, we should be attempting far more seriously than we are to lessen our present or future dependence on Arab or Iranian oil. This would allow us to pursue a more rational policy in the Middle East and to lessen our vulnerability to the Soviets in any case. In addition, it would free our nuclear policy from the burden of providing "extended" deterrence in the Middle East. Whatever one may think of them, there are at least some liberal-sounding reasons for providing extended deterrence to our allies in Western Europe. The case for risking nuclear war to protect oil supplies we should try to do without is certainly far weaker.

In fact, the inclination of American conservatives to exaggerate the threat of Communism and to sacrifice every other interest to "national security" touches on one of the deepest differences between liberals and conservatives. For, in the name of national security or anticommunism, conservatives have been willing to support regimes like those in South Africa and Argentina, and to destabilize or topple regimes like those in Chile and Guatemala. It is highly questionable whether the contribution to American or free world security can justify these actions, and it is certain that the worldwide appeal of America as the preeminent representative of liberal values has been gravely tarnished by these and similar actions. This is still more conspicuously the case whenever the notion of national security has been given an expansive reading that encompasses the defense of American interests beyond those reasonably associated with security. Liberals cannot accept, as much of the world has been unwilling to accept, the sacrifice of human rights to "secure" American economic interests and advantages. From a liberal point of view this willingness of the United States to sacrifice the liberal interests and rights of others is the profoundest failing of American foreign policy as it is a source of deep divergence between liberal and conservative approaches to foreign affairs. Not the least of its cost has been that it opens American opposition to the violation of human rights in the Soviet empire to the charge of opportunism and hypocrisy. Even now our approach to the Caribbean, to South Africa, and to Argentina has cost us significant support on the issue of Poland. The Soviet threat is real, but anticommunism, and certainly ill-focused anticommunism, cannot exhaust the liberal agenda.

Kant envisaged a perpetual peace instituted in a world of liberal states, and it has been a persistent theme of liberal thought from Kant to Woodrow Wilson that a world of republican states would be a peaceful one. Contemporary liberals may be more skeptical than traditional ones about the relation between domestic regimes and international conduct, but as Michael Doyle has argued, relations among the expanding company of liberal states has indeed constituted a sort of Kantian *foedus pacificum*.[16] In the period since World War II, the United States has provided impressive and largely successful leadership to this crucial alliance. The European allies, fearful of the Soviet threat and sheltered under the American nuclear "umbrella," achieved a unity unprecedented in modern European history. In addition, under the regime of the post-World War II economic institutions like the GATT and the IMF, the trade wars and beggar-thy-neighbor economic policies that aggravated the Depression of the thirties and contributed to the rise of antidemocratic politics were brought under control and a remarkable period of prosperity and cooperation, even of integration, ensued.

In the conditions that now face us this alliance has entered a period of testing and severe difficulty. It cannot be said that the present administration is handling these problems successfully. Its defense policies and its apparent attitude about the possibility of fighting a nuclear war have animated a disarmament movement that can only make the Russians more intractable in negotiations and that may ultimately threaten the NATO alliance itself. Equally disturbing are the likely consequences of the administration's economic policies, which, far from strengthening the alliance, are likely to damage it. The huge deficits, in part inspired by the desire for military strength, have raised interest rates to the point where they further weaken the European economies, already disabled by the oil crisis and the increasing rigors of international trade in a depressed world economy. A further slackening of these economies could well threaten the postwar achievements in economic cooperation and encourage antiliberal, extremist politics of the right and left. Certainly, they make it more difficult for European governments to honor or extend their military commitments. Neither our present military or economic policies toward Europe, nor those policies in the Middle East that affect European interests, inspire confidence in Europe and their only tendency can be to further fragment the liberal alliance.

The liberal world faces a cruel dilemma in its relations with Eastern Europe. European prosperity, and the prospect of ultimately undermining Soviet domination, can almost certainly be improved by weaving Eastern Europe, and even the Soviets, into the web of economic interdependence. But, as has become increasingly clear (it was already clear to Rousseau), greater interdependence means increased vulnerability. Realists are unquestionably correct, then, in urging that Europeans not become vulnerable to a Soviet cut-off of energy resources and that they not become so dependent on Eastern European trade that they are incapable of responding to Soviet threats and of influencing Soviet behavior in desirable directions.

At the moment there is room for disagreement among liberals as to whether shoring up Western European economies or punishing the Poles and Russians takes priority from a liberal point of view. It is certainly poor policy for the Reagan administration to cancel the grain embargo in deference to American economic interests while criticizing the Europeans for not taking more punitive measures. This posture can only add to our reputation for hypocrisy and empty rhetoric. All liberals must be outraged by the Russian tyranny over Eastern Europe, and they will not side with balance of power and sphere of influence realists who counsel us to acquiesce in it. I, myself, would support an even stronger response to the Polish outrage than the present administration has made. But an effective response would have required more consultation and planning within the alliance than the administration managed, and its chances of wide support would have been far greater if our concern for the prospects of liberty elsewhere were not so badly compromised. Certainly, effectiveness in these matters will require of us and of others a greater willingness to forgo economic benefits when we wish to advance the cause of liberty and justice in the world. If the Russians are more willing than we are to forgo the benefits of interdependence, it is *they* who will manipulate *us*. Increasingly, these issues will separate those who are committed to advancing liberal principles in the world from those who think that whether we do so or not is a question that can be answered only by consulting the oracle of the national interest. Liberals should refuse to sacrifice the liberties of others for their own prosperity.

The problems of developing a liberal policy toward the third world present the most difficult problems of all. Dilemmas appear which liberals of all sorts have difficulty in resolving, and differences between liberals and conservatives manifest themselves acutely in this area. The liberal norm is nonintervention, and it is scrupulously respected within the confines of the liberal world. Indeed, it is one of the central manifestations of the *foedus pacificum*. Mill has given the classic argument for the principle (and Michael Walzer the best recent discussion), founded on a people's right to self-determination.[17] The moral status of the rule against intervention is, however, far from absolute. There are obvious moral grounds for intervening against regimes whose excesses outrage the conscience of the world. And there are plainly liberal grounds for supporting political communities struggling for their independence from larger multiethnic or multinational communities as there are in counterinterventions in support of a liberal party when foreign forces have already intervened in support of the domestic tyranny it opposes.

With much of this Mill and Walzer would agree (although Mill does not mention humanitarian interventions and Walzer would permit counterinterventions only to restore the *status quo ante* and, apparently, for either side). But they argue on liberal grounds against interventions whose aim is to free oppressed populations from indigenous oppressors. Unless those in revolt are willing to make the sacrifices necessary to secure freedom for themselves, their love of liberty is suspect and the likelihood that they will maintain it slight. Therefore we do not in fact serve the interests of liberty by coming to their aid. But it ill suits those of us who prize a liberty we have not ourselves sacrificed very much to achieve to make victory against terrible odds the test either of the love of freedom or of the likelihood that once achieved it will be maintained.

Given the arsenals and technical skills of modern oppressors, it is often simply unrealistic to suppose that liberty can be achieved if enough people want it and want it badly. Surely, there is a strong liberal argument for intervention in cases of this sort as well. But if interventions (against native oppressors) in support of self-government and interventions (against foreign oppressors) in support of self-determination are attractive from a moral point of view, they both raise serious problems when proposed as practical principles of international conduct.[18] For one thing, the principles are easily abused. Unquestionably, it would be morally proper for us to counterintervene against the puppet regime in Afghanistan. But the Soviets claim it is we who intervene and they who counterintervene. Similar problems arise on our side. It is far from clear that in El Salvador (or that earlier in the Dominican Republic) there was a substantial, oppressive intervention to counter. And in Guatemala in 1954, it was disingenuous to claim that the CIA-led "army" that intervened against the Arbenz regime was a popular force liberating the Guatemalan people from an incipient Communist dictatorship.

One way to control the abuse of an exception is not to admit it, and there is, therefore, much to be said for upholding a strict interpretation of the rule of international law forbidding interventions, despite the incongruity it produces between what would otherwise be morally desirable and what is in fact legally workable. Certainly, a prohibition on interventions in recent years would have worked in the liberal interest. The main function of superpower interventions in recent years has been to control their respective spheres of interest or to contain those of their opponents, and not to secure the freedom of the peoples in whose affairs the superpowers intervened. This is obvious enough in the case of the Soviet interventions in Eastern Europe, but it is largely true of our own as well.

In addition to curbing the abuse of what on purely moral grounds are legitimate exceptions, the stronger rule would fortify the general legal prohibition on the use of force across borders. If we could in fact gain general conformity to this legal principle, our moral obligation to abide by a strict rule against intervention would, in all but extraordinary circumstances, outweigh the importance of acting within the exceptions.[19] We are, of course, far from that position, and given the Brezhnev doctrine the prospects of achieving it are, to put it mildly, unpromising. There is, nevertheless, much to be said for America's following a policy of great restraint in any case. The often intractable facts and the indelicacy and frequent brutality of American operations generally make our well-intentioned interventions failures. Even when the foreign politicians we support genuinely favor liberal objectives they are often unable to deliver on them. In providing these leaders with support we open them to the charge of being puppets of American imperialism and compromise our own reputation as they turn increasingly authoritarian and repressive.[20] Frequently, as in Guatemala, we produce more violent extremes than we faced in the first place and reinforce the widespread view that those we support favor our economic interests, promise "stability," or promote our geopolitical strategies.

In view of all this, a policy of restraint would probably enhance, not only our own reputation as a nation devoted to international law and to the liberties of men, but the actual prospects for a more stable, law-abiding, and liberal world as well. This is not to say that a more fastidious and genuinely liberal America should be reluctant to provide aid short of military intervention to those fighting for freedom. And in the absence of reciprocity there will be occasions, as in the case of the Spanish civil war, when military intervention would not only be justifiable but highly desirable. In the case of counterinterventions, at least, Mill was right when he wrote, "The doctrine of non-intervention, to be a legitimate principle of morality, must be accepted by all governments. The despots must consent to be bound by it as well as the free States. Unless they do, the profession of it by free countries comes but to this miserable issue, that the wrong side may help the wrong but the right must not help the right."[21]

Further dilemmas of liberal policy toward the third world arise in connection with the demand for a new economic order. Some conservatives think that our response to this demand should be guided simply by considerations of prudence and self-interest, and their practical policies reflect their estimates of how damaging an unappeased third world can actually be to our long-run economic interests. Other conservatives concede that issues of justice are at stake, but insist that, to a considerable degree, the distributions of the market satisfy (some even say define) the requirements of justice.

By contrast, liberals think that simple humanitarian requirements, not to mention the claims of justice, are much more demanding. (This is, incidentally, one reason why a liberal foreign policy must attempt to alter the international order and cannot plausibly confine itself to the task of building an exemplary liberal society in moral or practical isolation from others.) But in seeking to meet the requirements of humanitarian aid and just distribution, liberal states come up against the fact that the state remains the fundamental actor in the present international system. For some third world spokesmen the principles of sovereignty or of state equality are incompatible with a liberal policy that attempts to penetrate the shell of state sovereignty and to impose distributive requirements on it.[22] As Brian Barry puts it, the requirement of justice is "that countries, as collectivities, should have their fair share of the world's resources" and this claim must be satisfied, whatever the realities of internal distribution may be.[23]

Unquestionably, some deference must be paid to the principles of sovereignty in question for under the present circumstances individual self-respect is at least indirectly related to national self-respect. But, while these principles must be acknowledged, it is necessary to subordinate them to principles directing humanitarian aid and just shares to individuals. A fundamental impulse of liberal morality is to relieve the suffering of individuals quite aside from any requirements of justice (and this principle alone would require far greater sacrifices than are now made by the wealthier nations). Surely, when resources are transferred on this basis it is proper to insist that they serve their intended purpose.[24] But liberals also believe that transfers should be made to satisfy the claims of justice, and these claims are, fundamentally, the claims of individuals, not of collectivities. It is a central conviction of liberals that there is something unfair about social arrangements that confer such radically different prospects of health, education, productivity, and personal autonomy on those who are born into different societies.

It is this situation that liberal transfers aim to mitigate, and it is difficult to see why these transfers should be made if they will be used by domestic leaders to entrench their own illegitimate authority or in ways that do not ameliorate but perhaps even aggravate the situation they are intended to improve. Insofar as transfer policies are understood to implement requirements of justice, there is much to be said for channeling them through broadly representative international institutions on a "nonpolitical" basis. However that may be, just claims cannot be denied simply because of political differences with those who make them. It is worth remembering, however, that there will always be aspects of international economic behavior that are dictated neither by principles of humanity nor by the requirements of justice, and here we are certainly free to establish special relationships with those we favor or with whom we have a moral affinity. We may favor those whom we hope to attract into the Kantian alliance of liberal states.

The present administration is too confused in the formulation and the execution of its policies for confident judgments or predictions to be made, but from a liberal point of view it promises to be profoundly disappointing. One might have expected the present administration to be most effective in resisting Soviet purposes; however, instead of focusing the world's attention on Soviet outrages, it has to a large extent shifted that attention to its own alarming military policies and rhetoric. The administration has provided ineffective leadership on the Polish issue and has, if anything, weakened the already troubled alliance of liberal states. Its attitude toward the third world seems dictated mainly by a narrow conception of the national interest and by often implausible geopolitical considerations. Its concern for liberty (and even for its own impoverished conception of justice) is weak and unpersuasive. Many of its faults derive from internal incoherence and technical confusion. But they derive, as well, from its particular kind of conservative orientation. Its policies and attitudes constitute an unfortunate deviation from liberal principles and will undermine still further America's ability to lead the free world or to inaugurate a more liberal one.

Notes

1. John Rawls, "A Kantian Conception of Equality," *Cambridge Review* (February 1975):94–95.

2. Ronald Dworkin, "Liberalism," in *Public and Private Morality*, edited by Stuart Hampshire (Cambridge: Cambridge University Press, 1978), pp. 113–43.

3. Isaiah Berlin, *Four Essays on Liberty* (Oxford: Oxford University Press, 1969), pp. 129–31. For a criticism of this position, see Marshall Cohen, "Berlin and the Liberal Tradition," *Philosophical Quarterly* 10, no. 40 (July 1960):216–27.

4. R. B. Mowat, *Public and Private Morality* (Bristol: Arrowsmith, 1933), p. 40.

5. Quoted by Hans Morgenthau, *Scientific Man vs. Power Politics* (Chicago: The University of Chicago Press, 1974), p. 180.

6. Hans Morgenthau, *In Defence of the National Interest* (New York: Alfred A. Knopf, 1952), p. 62. For a brief discussion of Morgenthau's realism, see Marshall Cohen, "The Humanities and the Modern," *Humanities in Society* 1, no. 1 (1978):8–11.

7. Morgenthau, *Scientific Man vs. Power Politics*, p. 60.

8. Robert Jervis, "Cooperation Under the Security Dilemma," *World Politics* 30, no. 2 (January 1978):167–214. The entire paragraph, and much else in my discussion, is drawn from this article.

9. David Gauthier, *The Logic of Leviathan* (Oxford: Oxford University Press, 1969), p. 208. This quotation needs to be considered in the context of Gauthier's full discussion.

10. Jervis, "Cooperation Under the Security Dilemma," p. 212.

11. Thomas C. Schelling, *The Strategy of Conflict* (Oxford and New York: Oxford University Press, 1971), p. 232.

12. Jervis, "Cooperation Under the Security Dilemma," pp. 181–82.

13. Immanuel Kant, *The Philosophy of Law*, translated by W. Hastie (Edinburgh: T. and T. Clark, 1887), pp. 229–30. Quoted by Kenneth N. Waltz, "Kant, Liberalism, and War," *The American Political Science Review* 56, no. 2 (June 1962):331–40.

14. McGeorge Bundy et al., "Nuclear Weapons and the Atlantic Alliance," *Foreign Affairs* 60, no. 4 (Spring 1982):753–68.

15. Colin Gray and Keith Payne, "Victory Is Possible," *Foreign Policy* 39 (Summer 1980):21.

16. Michael Doyle, "Kant, Liberal Legacies and Foreign Affairs," *Philosophy & Public Affairs* 12, nos. 3 and 4 (Summer and Fall 1983). I am much indebted to this article for a number of important suggestions.

17. J. S. Mill, "A Few Words on Non-Intervention," *Dissertations and Discussions III* (London: Longmans, Green, & Company, 1867), pp. 153–78. Michael Walzer, *Just and Unjust Wars* (New York: Basic Books, 1977), pp. 86–108.

18. Stanley Hoffman, *Duties Beyond Borders* (Syracuse, N.Y.: Syracuse University Press, 1981), pp. 62–73.

19. Marshall Cohen, "Morality and Military Intervention," in *The Proceedings of the War and Morality Symposium*, edited by Robert H. Rains and Michael J. McRae (West Point: United States Military Academy, 1980), pp. 48–52.

20. Stanley Hoffman, *Gulliver's Troubles, Or the Setting of American Foreign Policy* (New York: McGraw–Hill, 1968), p. 200ff. I am also undoubtedly indebted to other of Professor Hoffman's many writings on this subject.

21. Mill, "A Few Words," p. 176.

22. Robert W. Tucker, *The Inequality of Nations* (New York: Basic Books, 1977), p. 58ff.

23. Brian Barry, "Justice as Reciprocity," in *Justice*, edited by Eugene Kamenka and Alice Erh-Soon Tay (New York: St. Martin's Press, 1980), p. 77.

24. Ibid., p. 77.

6

The Legacies of New Deal Liberalism

THEDA SKOCPOL

The United States, as Louis Hartz argues in *The Liberal Tradition in America*, may have been born liberal, and it may have grown up over two centuries confined within an unself-conscious Lockean consensus about an "American way of life" based on private property, individual freedom, and equality of opportunity for everyone to race ahead in the free market unencumbered by state controls.[1] Nevertheless, "liberalism" as an explicit political stance defined in opposition to "conservatism" emerged only during the New Deal of the 1930s—ironically, at the very historical moment when U.S. politics was pushing beyond the anti-statist presumptions of classical liberalism.

During the grave crisis of the Depression, Franklin Roosevelt needed a new political label to symbolize the "bold, persistent experimentation" of the New Deal. His new program called for the federal government to intervene in markets and society to promote the rights and welfare of nonprivileged groups and to ensure socioeconomic security and political stability for the nation as a whole. As the careful research of Ronald Rotunda has demonstrated, Roosevelt and other New Dealers deliberately chose the "liberal" label over possible alternatives: Prior to the 1930s, "liberalism" had been used occasionally as a synonym for "progressivism." It could tap progressive support yet still symbolize innovative departures. "Liberalism" was also a good alternative and antidote to "socialism," allowing New Dealers to parry accusations of bureaucratic coercion and rigid collectivism, while competing with Herbert Hoover and other conservative critics of the New Deal for the claim of best representing the traditional American values of individualism and liberty.[2] Their governmental activism, New Deal liberals asserted, better protected democratic liberties and individual well-being and opportunity than did the cold-hearted, laissez-faire pieties of conservatism. In short, as Sam Beer sums up:

[I]t is from the New Deal that liberalism in its contemporary American usage has acquired its principal meaning. . . . The liberalism that has been a really significant power in American politics, both as a set of ideas and a social force, has been . . . the *practical liberalism* [emphasis mine] brought into existence by the New Deal. And the stress on economic balance and economic security that was characteristic of the New Deal remained essential to the meaning of liberalism in its later embodiments in Truman's Fair Deal and the programs of the Kennedy-Johnson administrations.[3]

Indeed, from the 1940s through the mid-1970s, it appeared that this "practical liberalism" of the New Deal had irreversibly established the terms and limits of debate for domestic national politics. I do not mean to suggest, of course, that Democratic Party liberals continuously held power or usually got their way. There were the Republican presidencies of Eisenhower and Nixon, and the conservative congressional coalition of Republicans and Southern Democrats defeated quite a few liberal initiatives (and eviscerated many others), even when liberal Democrats sat in the White House. All the same, from 1940 onward even most Republicans and conservatives accepted the inevitability of basic New Deal accomplishments, such as Social Security, legalized labor unions, federal farm-price supports, and housing and urban-development subsidies. Arguments were not over *whether* the government should undertake basic "positive" programs, but over the details of *how* government should act (e.g., direct federal controls versus indirect subsidies to private actors or to local and state governments), of *who should benefit* (e.g., middle-class suburbanites and well-to-do commercial farmers versus the poor), and of *how federal expenditures should be financed* (e.g., deficit spending versus increased taxes, and taxes of what sorts, collected from whom?).

Certainly, post-New Deal liberals and conservatives struggled over many important issues between 1940 and the mid-1970s, and conservative victories stymied or modified most liberal initiatives. But it was still a comfortable, complacent era for the heirs of New Deal practical liberalism. All of the battles were, so to speak, on their terrain, and in politics, as in warfare, advantages of terrain count for a great deal. They can insure against losing the war even when many engagements are forfeited. During the entire era from the Fair Deal through (and beyond) the Great Society, "practical liberals" could face defeats, set-backs, and partial victories with equanimity for they determined the issues around which the battles would be fought. After bandaging their wounds, resting their forces, and (they hoped) bringing up reinforcements through victories in the next election, they would surely return to fight again another day.

Well, now, in the early 1980s, post-New Deal practical liberals can no longer be so complacent. The terrain of American political battles has suddenly shifted, and modern U.S. liberalism—the New

Deal's commitment to social and economic betterment through partial, gradually extended federal government interventions—has suddenly come into question, especially from a resurgent new right, but also from an occasionally heard democratic-socialist left. Not surprisingly, the New Deal figures prominently in the current debates about where America should go politically from here. This is not just because 1982 was the centennial of Franklin Delano Roosevelt's birth, but also because spokespersons of all political persuasions rightly sense that the era of New Deal liberalism is coming either to an end or to a fundamental watershed.

Yet the New Deal still resonates so potently in the American public imagination that virtually everyone involved in reexamining the legacy of practical liberalism is, at the same time, trumpeting an intention to recapture (or continue) the New Deal's true spirit. Thus, from the anti-welfare-state right, Ronald Reagan tells us that FDR was, at heart, a budget-balancer reluctant to extend government handouts to the poor beyond strictly temporary "relief," for fear of permanently undermining the moral fiber of the American people. And from the socialist left, Alan Wolfe tells us in his provocative and important recent book, *America's Impasse*, that New Deal liberalism lost its soul only in the aftermath of World War II, when Democrats failed to reassert the genuine New Deal program of government planning and income redistribution.[4] Finally, today's "liberal" Democrats (although not sure that they want to call themselves that anymore!) are groping for tactics to continue practical liberalism in the new climate.

Much of what *The New Republic* has to say these days embodies this effort, and according to that journal's recent editorial reexamination of Roosevelt, his "largeness of democratic spirit" is what today's Democratic Party should continue. It shouldn't become a party of minorities, hung up on socioeconomic redistribution, but should imitate Roosevelt's "inclusiveness and universality of . . . social vision" by respecting "the real discontents of the American middle class—the fear of crime, the disgust with lousy schools, the creeping sense of social and economic disintegration" and by emphasizing, in response, policies of "human capital" development, of "equality of opportunity," and of limits on bureaucracy to cement the link between the Democratic Party and that broad American "middle-class."[5] In sum, much as Roosevelt himself in the 1930s hoped to capitalize upon the ambiguous resonances of the liberal label with progressivism and with liberty, contemporary U.S. political innovators try to avoid the appearance of fundamental ideological departures by claiming to reconnect with what was best about the New Deal, even as they discard the undesirable or outmoded tenets of practical liberalism as it came down to us from that era.

My own view about the connection between the New Deal and the political choices Americans in and to the left of the Democratic

Party now face is rather more hard-headed and less sentimental than the views of any of those trying to define and recapture the New Deal's true spirit. While the New Deal is certainly responsible for many of the best things that have been achieved in twentieth-century U.S. politics (with the crucial exception of the civil rights breakthroughs of the 1960s) it is now time to dissect its flawed achievements, its failed possibilities, and its contradictory unintended legacies. We must come to understand exactly why the practical liberalism of the New Deal was never politically coherent or self-sustaining in its own terms. Once this is done, we should be able to see the best way forward for defending and building upon the New Deal's achievements—achievements such as establishing federal government responsibility for socioeconomic security and national economic well-being, and extending new benefits to the socially and politically excluded. The way forward will require much more ideologically and politically coherent choices than any that might be embodied in either a romantic return to the spirit of the 1930s or a slightly refurbished version of New Deal and post-New Deal practical liberalism propounded by an unreorganized version of today's Democratic Party.

The Political Failings of the
Domestic New Deal, 1932–1939

It is by now a commonplace that the New Deal failed to bring full national economic recovery to America. That came only with World War II. And everyone would agree that, since recovery was one of the New Deal's most persistently declared objectives, it was, even in its own terms, an economic failure. Less often recognized but equally significant are the *political* shortcomings of the New Deal. They are obscured because World War II brought America international triumphs and national economic expansion. Yet as the heading for a recent magazine article cleverly put it: "Between Dr. New Deal and Dr. Win-the-War was Dr. Stalemate."[6] From 1937 to 1940 Franklin Roosevelt had to use all of his personal political skills to ride out a period of repeated defeats for his domestic (and international) political program.

In the 1932, 1934, and 1936 elections, Roosevelt's increasingly reformist New Deal programs scored a succession of ever-greater electoral triumphs. By 1936, the New Deal electoral base had expanded to a degree unprecedented in twentieth-century America; this support was truly national and proportionately stronger as one descended the socioeconomic scale.[7] After the 1936 election, FDR and the Democratic-dominated Congress were ostensibly set to launch a series of programs to extend and securely institutionalize the social reforms of the Second New Deal. But these efforts faltered from the very start: Roosevelt's plans for "reforming" the Supreme Court and for reorganizing the executive branch were stymied; redistributive spending measures were increasingly trimmed back; an extension of TVA-style regional planning was defeated; and key programs favoring labor, poorer farmers, blacks, and consumers of low-cost housing were blocked or severely circumscribed by conservatives in Congress.[8] Then, from the 1938 election on through 1946, New Deal liberals lost regular increments of electoral support. Roosevelt squeaked into World War II just ahead of the anti-union, anti-New Deal Communist hunters in Congress. Although many core New Deal reforms, such as legalizing labor unions, were solidly institutionalized during World War II, many others were eliminated by Congress during or immediately after the war, especially those moving toward national social and economic planning, extended welfare provisions and guarantees of national full employment, and help for poorer farmers, farm tenants, and farm laborers.[9] Essentially, all of the New Deal's significant post-1936 redistributive and state-strengthening efforts were stymied or trimmed away during the very period from 1937 to 1946 when Roosevelt secured his personally triumphant place in the annals of the U.S. presidency, and when the practical liberalism of the Democratic Party came to set the terms and limits of discourse for U.S. politics in the middle twentieth century.

What happened to the reformist New Deal immediately after 1936? Why didn't the huge electoral triumph translate into greater and sustained momentum for further socioeconomic redistribution, for broader planning, and for well-institutionalized, social-democratic Keynesian styles of government taxing and spending? Many historians would point to FDR's poor tactics in attacking the Supreme Court when and how he did, or would argue that the American electorate didn't really want further New Deal reforms. While there may be correct insights in these explanations, both fail to underline the more important *constraints of U.S. governmental structure and of Democratic Party organization* that underlay the sudden stalling of the domestic New Deal between 1936 and 1939. Although neither FDR nor "urban liberal" New Dealers fully knew or willingly accepted it (that is why they kept *trying* to do reformist things), the New Deal by 1936 had squeezed just about all of the sociopolitical innovations it could out of the existing U.S. political structures. And indeed, through its own earlier achievements and initiatives, it had set in motion within the bounds of those structures counterforces that would stop further progress and erode the enduring foundations of liberal reforms.

Let me spell out what I mean in a bit more detail by talking briefly about three key areas of political failure in the New Deal, suggesting how the structures of U.S. government and of the Democratic Party helped produce these shortcomings. Dealing in turn with the New Deal's popular political support, its attempts at governmental reorganization, and its ideological rationale for the emergent American welfare state, I will briefly discuss important failures to achieve very real possibilities that were implicit in the New Deal's distinctive political support or present in concrete policies advocated by FDR himself and other prominent New Deal officials.

THE NEW DEAL FAILED TO CREATE A STABLE POLITICAL COALITION BETWEEN FARMERS AND URBAN WORKERS.

Anyone who reads through FDR's political speeches in the early 1930s can see that he was trying to make the Democratic Party appealing to both farmers and urban workers. He often stressed ways in which the economic welfare of nonprivileged urban and rural Americans was tied together. Ironically, however, New Deal agricultural policies ended up politically strengthening conservative rural interests, which would from 1936 onward oppose many key elements of urban-liberal programs favoring unionized workers and the poor. The early New Deal's major effort to raise farm prices, the Agricultural Adjustment Act, was successfully implemented largely with preexisting federal government resources, such as the U.S. Department of Agriculture and the federal-state Extension Service.[10] An unintended effect was to greatly strengthen the American Farm Bureau Federation (AFBF), an interest group based especially on richer commercial farmers in the South and Midwest.[11] Because of this group's increasingly effective lobbying, and because Roosevelt was never willing to antagonize Southern Democrats in Congress, New Deal agricultural programs to help black tenants in the cotton South, or poorer farmers anywhere, were shunted to the margins of the New Deal and ultimately whittled away and destroyed by Congress between 1937 and 1945.[12] No sooner, moreover, had richer farmers recovered from the worst Depression ravages with New Deal aid (something they did by 1936) than they and their congressional representatives began to turn against further New Deal reforms. Thus, just as liberal, urban-based Democrats hit their legislative stride in 1936, they faced decreasing rural support for their programs.[13] Had blacks in the South been able to vote, or had earlier New Deal farm programs strengthened organizations representing tenants or poorer farmers, a strong urban/rural liberal coalition might have locked into place by 1936. As it was, however, the USDA's and the Extension Service's symbiotic ties to the AFBF, and the politically expedient efforts of early New Deal farm programs to avoid ruffling the feathers of congressional Democrats elected by the cotton planter-influenced white oligarchies of the South, proved too effective. These unchallenged "givens" of the federal administrative structure and of Congress and the Democratic Party channeled the New Deal away from the farmer/worker coalition implicit in its electoral appeals and implicit in the enthusiastic support the New Deal received in 1932, 1934, and 1936 from poorer farmers and workers in the United States as a whole.

THE NEW DEAL FAILED TO LINK ITS "URBAN-LIBERAL" REFORMS TO AN INSTITUTIONALIZED SYSTEM OF FEDERAL ECONOMIC PLANNING.

From 1935 to 1938, a number of "urban-liberal" measures passed that created new bases of political support for New Deal liberals and mandated permanent flows of social spending. Examples include the Wagner Act (which legalized labor unions), the Social Security Act (which provided federal welfare subsidies and established old-age and unemployment insurance), the Wagner Housing bill, and continuing appropriations for public works and emergency relief. By the time of the 1937 recession, moreover, many New Dealers, including the ever-reluctant FDR, were somewhat persuaded that Keynesian-style federal deficit spending could help achieve economic recovery and sustained economic growth.

What the U.S. federal executive government of the 1930s sorely lacked, though, was established administrative capacity to plan social and economic programs and to coordinate and implement them through functionally streamlined federal agencies. During the New Deal, academic experts presented Roosevelt with ideas for permanent, authoritative organs of national and regional planning.[14] He responded favorably to a number of concrete proposals and translated them into legislation or executive agencies. Still, unless various planning agencies could be linked to strong executive controls over budgeting, administration, and spending, they would mean little in practice.

However, FDR's comprehensive executive reorganization scheme, drawn up by professionals interested in social and economic planning and introduced after the 1936 election, was defeated in Congress. Congressional representatives, cabinet officials, and established interest groups were all afraid to disrupt their established mutual relationships, their little "iron triangles" of votes traded for piecemeal legislative benefits.[15] Even key urban liberals like Robert Wagner opposed the very executive reorganization that might have made social-democratic spending and planning possible because he feared for the "independence" of the National Labor Relations Board as a semi-autonomous bureaucracy.

Unfortunately, those advocating national or regional planning in the New Deal period (and after) were never very realistic about how to fit their schemes into the existing U.S. political system.[16] They often advocated regional planning agencies because they hoped to bypass "politics" altogether, i.e., by avoiding Congress, local urban machines, and the states, all in the name of "expert authority" and "neutral administrative efficiency." Planning advocates were, in part, hampered by an illusion of the professional middle class carried into the New Deal from the Progressive Era. The illusion was that good administration and wise planning could not go along with democratic politics.[17] Progressive Era reforms had fought patronage-oriented, popular-democratically based machines. In the New Deal, it might have been possible to garner a new kind of national democratic support for planning, especially for a goal like full employment. But expert planning advocates instead tried to stay away from "politics" as something implicitly dirty and contrary to their aims. Hence they failed to achieve stable support for planning agencies. And eventually, in the early 1940s, Congress destroyed the last of the comprehensive planning boards set up by FDR; ironically, soon after it published a comprehensive social-democratic Keynesian plan for *Security, Work, and Relief Policies* to be implemented by liberal Democrats after the war![18]

THE NEW DEAL FAILED TO LEGITIMATE NEW NATIONAL WELFARE PROGRAMS IN COMMUNAL TERMS.

In an excellent essay called "The New Deal and the American Anti-Statist Tradition," James Holt has analyzed the evolving symbols and arguments invoked by New Dealers during the 1930s to characterize and justify their new federal economic interventions and welfare reforms. Holt explores the extent to which "the difficulty of explaining and defending a complex and novel program of federal action in the face of deeply entrenched anti-statist traditions impeded the Roosevelt administration's efforts at reform."[19] The New Deal was up against anti-statist tradition in the 1930s not just because Americans were ideologically prejudiced against strong, sovereign, public authority but also because, historically, they had not experienced (for good or ill) the impact of policies implemented by a centralized, bureaucratic national state. In nineteenth-century America, there was no such thing, and even though federal administrative activities did expand markedly in the twentieth century, Congress and the federal system always circumscribed direct, coordinated "national state" activities.[20] Americans thought of practical sovereignty as divided, and of ultimate sovereignty as residing abstractly in "the law" and "the Constitution," because these ideas in fact made the best sense possible of the actual conditions of political organization and action with which they lived.[21]

But FDR's New Deal made direct federal governmental activities an immediate reality for all Americans, and *the justification and portrayal of these new programs in New Deal rhetoric was a portentous ideological development in U.S. history.* As Holt shows, in the early

New Deal, FDR and his fellow politicians relied heavily on images of cooperation, combined with constant stress on the "experimental" activism of New Deal efforts. Things had to be done to promote economic recovery and relieve distress; only a distant, heartless federal government would fail to act boldly, and FDR's government would "roll up its sleeves" and "keep them rolled up," acting in the name of neighborliness to bring the whole nation together in response to the emergency. As Holt astutely points out, this early New Deal rhetoric, although rather thin and expedient in many ways, did have a component of moral regeneration. For New Dealers called upon Americans to put aside selfish, competitive individualism in the name of solidarity and cooperation across sectional and class lines.

However, as the early New Deal (launched around the ultimately unsuccessful National Recovery Administration) gave way to the second, reformist New Deal of 1935 and after, its rhetoric changed. It became more focused on *political conflict* (the people against the "economic royalists") and on *social security* for "the one-third of a Nation ill-fed, ill-housed, ill-clothed," not to mention the many still unemployed. In these ways, the rhetoric of the by-now explicitly "liberal" New Deal became undeniably more radical. But, as James Holt underlines, in another way it simultaneously became more conservative. The New Dealers after 1935 mostly gave up the rhetoric of collective solidarity as an antidote to excessive individualism, and instead sought to justify New Deal reforms as better means for achieving or safeguarding traditional American values of liberty and individualism. Their nascent national welfare state, New Dealers told Americans, was not the attack on basic American values that conservatives were saying it was, rather merely an excellent instrument for furthering those values by avoiding anarchy or dictatorship in the Depression crisis, striking down the excessive privileges and power of "economic autocrats," and relieving economic necessity so that Americans in distress could really be free and exercise their rights to equality of opportunity.

Now, obviously, New Dealers turned to this *instrumental* justification for their welfare-state reforms, tying them to established values of healthy market capitalism, individual rights, and equality of opportunity, precisely because New Dealers felt ideologically pressured from the right from 1934 on. They were operating in an individualist and anti-statist political system, and they were facing increasingly vociferous conservative opponents with many political levers at their disposal in Congress and in the Democratic (and Republican) parties. Just as the comfortable ambiguities of the word "liberal" were a convenient way for the New Dealers to defuse rightist criticism, so was an essentially instrumentalist strategy for legitimating the new "practical liberal" welfare state.

In fact, it is possible, even probable, that the instrumental approach to legitimating the new state activities established by the New Deal actually was the safest way to stabilize and modestly extend "practical liberal" policies in U.S. domestic politics between 1937 and 1975. Between 1937 and 1940, liberal New Dealers were not able to beat conservatives in head-on collisions, and during and after World War II, liberal Democratic gains generally depended upon taking advantage of the rosy climate of national economic expansion and U.S. international hegemony to push through some reformist measures along with national spending programs. These would benefit not only blue-collar workers and the poor but also the more "middle class," more suburban, and richer supporters of the Republicans. In these political circumstances, noncollectivist visions of liberalism and the welfare state were no doubt the only rhetorically workable ones.

Basically, to have achieved more of the essentially social-democratic goals that they began to strive for in the post-1936 New Deal, New Deal liberals should have been much less "practical" than they were *at the very start of their period of power*. Roosevelt should have attempted a liberal reorganization of the Democratic Party from 1933 to 1936, rather than waiting (as he did) to make a feeble, thoroughly unsuccessful effort in 1938. All New Dealers, especially urban-liberals, should have striven from the start to make structural changes in Southern agriculture and race relations, and through these to reform and liberalize, indeed revolutionize, the Southern wing of the Democratic Party. Would-be planners and reorganizers of the federal government should have tried to make explicit popular political appeals in 1934 to 1936. And New Dealers should have clothed their positive federal actions throughout in rhetoric combining class appeals and visions of national socioeconomic security with explicit new definitions of *state action as a desirable and enduringly necessary instrument of national public good* as well as individual well-being. People's inevitable dependence upon one another and upon a healthy public life should have been stressed to legitimize welfare efforts.

Now, of course, I am not denying that there were many historical factors at work to make the New Deal happen the way it actually did. It is still useful, however, to set up the ideal counterfactual scenario, not only because it suggests how history might have unfolded differently, but also because it may help us to understand the problematic legacies that New Deal liberalism has bequeathed to us now that the comfortable 1940 to 1975 interlude of steady U.S. national economic growth and international hegemony is over. For now, in the 1980s, the chickens of the New Deal's flawed accomplishments are coming home to roost. To deal with the hard political choices that are upon us, we must become as clear as possible about what harm (as well as good) the New Deal's timid practical liberalism may have done. And we must learn as much as possible from the

New Deal reformers' political blind-spots and strategic failures in order to see how reformers today might do better if they ever get another chance to try.

The End of New Deal Liberalism and Where to Go From Here

A recent *Chicago Tribune* column by feature-writer Anne Keegan, entitled "New Deal Has a Fit of Depression," highlights the contradictory legacies of New Deal liberalism in one small Texas town.[22] New Deal, Texas ("a town where just about everyone makes his living off cotton farming") did not exist back in the 1930s.

> It was merely a stop along the railroad where cotton was loaded up to be shipped off to the mills. . . .
> "No dwellings at all," says Ora May Hindman, the town's self-appointed historian. "Nothing around here but family farms."
> But then came the Depression. And Roosevelt. And the New Deal.
> "Back in the Depression when nobody had much of anything and no jobs and Roosevelt was handing out money," says Zo Clary, the school assessor, "he handed out some this way. And they built a consolidated schoolhouse right here, and they called it New Deal. People moved in, and the town grew up around it."

Cotton farming was good over the next several decades, in an era of national growth, with price-supports in place. Fathers did well and passed on prosperous family spreads to sons. But now another economic depression has hit, and bankruptcies are spreading in New Deal.

> The bad economy, the low prices for cotton, the inflated cost of farm equipment, the high cost of fuel and the prohibitive interest on bank loans—and farmers live on loans until the harvest comes in—are breaking these farmers.

And how do the threatened denizens of New Deal interpret their situation? Anne Keegan reports:

> Not only are these long-time cotton farmers afraid of being forced to go broke, sell out and maybe lose their cherished land, they are also afraid of what that will mean—the extinction of the *independent farmer*. . . . [emphasis mine]
> If there is fear among these men now, and pessimism and even an uncharacteristic cynicism—it is not directed toward Ronald Reagan, their president.
> "Hell, what he is contending with is what we saw building up and coming at us for years," mutters one of the farmers. "Too many handouts in this country. Too much something for nothing. Food stamps, welfare, federal programs growing bigger.

"Too much bureaucracy. Too much getting soft and lazy. That's what led us to this. Reagan is trying but he's fighting a building up over the years. He can't turn it around overnight. He's doing what has to be done. And about time, by God."

Roosevelt may have poured money into New Deal back in the old depression and done the town some good, but that's not what these farmers want for New Deal in this the new depression.

"Just the opposite," says one of them. "We don't want handouts. We don't want food stamps or welfare. We just want a little help in having the interest rates dropped down for farmers. . . ."

These reactions from Texas cotton farmers, whose town was built upon New Deal public works and cotton price supports, and who now oppose government spending, welfare, and bureaucracy, and merely want federal interest subsidies for farmers, also echo among blue-collar unionists and middle-class suburbanites formerly and currently helped by practical liberal programs ranging from the Wagner Act to home mortgage subsidies. The unionists want particular jobs in particular industries saved through federal bail-outs but oppose "welfare handouts." The middle-class suburbanites want college loans preserved but oppose "bureaucratic quotas" enforcing affirmative action for blacks. And so forth.

The basic political shortcomings of the New Deal's practical liberalism matter very much now that federal spending does not appear to guarantee a healthy economy and a steadily growing pie of revenues and opportunities from which every interest group can benefit with no hard public choices. The absence of strong political coalitions across urban and rural, black and white, middle class and poor is glaringly apparent. The absence of authoritative governmental centers for national economic planning and for the coordination of social and economic interventions makes continued confidence in federal "bureaucratic meddling" difficult to sustain. And most obvious and dangerous of all is the incomprehension of all too many Americans that, as Michael Walzer eloquently puts it, "the welfare state . . . expresses a certain civil spirit, a sense of mutuality, a commitment to justice. Without that sense, no society can survive for long as a decent place to live—not for the needy, and not for anyone else." Walzer continues:

The idea of the welfare state isn't exhausted by a modest effort at income redistribution, risk control, relief for the poor, and health and employment insurance. The word "welfare" means "the state or condition of well-being,"and well-being is a moral as well as a material condition. Communal provision is required for the whole range of social goods that make up what we think of as our way of life. Not my way of life or yours, but ours, the life we couldn't have if we didn't plan for it and pay for it together. Not subsistence only, but science, culture, schooling, communication, travel, natural beauty: all this is public business. . . . The ideology of selfishness has no answer to the question, how shall *we* live?[23]

Unfortunately, given the legacies of the New Deal's political shortcomings, Reaganite proponents of the ideology of selfishness are having an easy time attacking practical liberalism from its right flank. Incoherent, piecemeal government regulations and subsidies may promote partial securities for mutually isolated interest groups, each of which will fiercely defend its own government programs. But they do not add up to the reality or the appearance of effective public planning for societal health or national economic readjustment in an era of crisis. Nor can the welfare state—the entire collection of programs for public goods and programs expressing social compassion and solidarity—be easily defended against individualist, market-oriented, anti-statist attacks when it lacks clear political and cultural legitimation.

What are practical liberalism's direct heirs, especially the denizens of the Democratic Party, doing about the crises of their governmental system and their long-taken-for-granted political creed? As one possible indication, *The New Republic's* recent special issue offering "ideas, themes, and proposals that the Democratic Party ought to be debating as it looks toward 1984 and beyond," suggests that they may be far from thinking radically enough. *The New Republic* suggests a refurbishment and continuation of long-established "liberal and democratic values," and declares that the "challenge after Reagan remains what it has always been, to make those values the living substance of our common life."[24]

Nowhere in *The New Republic* special issue, including the distinctly social-democratic articles by Michael Walzer, Lester Thurow, and Robert B. Reich, do we find any mention of a need for basic *political reforms* such as federal government restructuring, reorganization of the Democratic Party, mobilization of new political alliances, or reexamination of the basic practical liberal values, public rhetoric, or ideological self-understandings with which the Democratic Party has long been operating. Thurow complains briefly about the misguided industrial policies adopted by congressional representatives anxious simply to preserve existing jobs and companies in their districts, no matter how economically inefficient.[25] But when he and Reich call for new regional public investment banks, they, like the Progressives and New Deal academic planning proponents of old, say nary a word about how, politically, to fit these into the existing or a reorganized system of American democratic government. In his eloquent moral defense of the communal values of "the welfare state—taxes, bureaucrats, rules and regulations—the whole thing," Walzer mentions the steady decline in U.S. political participation.[26] Yet he has nothing practical to say about how to mobilize and organize

new levels of political participation or how to inspire morally reed-
ucated public commitment to the welfare state. Are we to believe
that the existing Democratic Party—with its recent reforms partly
revoked to strengthen the hand of already elected party officials—
can serve as an adequate organizational and ideological vehicle for
creating, enacting, and supporting a social-democratic vision of the
welfare state, not to mention planned national economic renewal?
The notion really strains the imagination.

Much more likely is that any unreformed Democratic Party that
comes back to power after an immediate Republican/Reagan debacle
in 1984 will do no more (and, really, *aim* to do no more) than
reinstate or slightly extend the old, pre-1980 practical liberal measures
of federal social spending, especially those wanted most by the white-
collar and professional middle classes: college loans, research monies,
environmental programs, and federal programs for the arts and for
urban development. Nor would anything more than defensive, status-
quo-oriented programs of security for declining industries seem at
all likely from the existing Democratic Party working through the
existing structures of congressional representation. Since none of this
would address the fundamentals of the current U.S. economic crisis
or mobilize significant new support for the Democratic Party, the
rightist critique of the old practical liberalism would probably remain
strong, perhaps sweeping neo-Reaganites, or worse, back into power
after a few years.

Back in 1976, *Commentary* magazine ran a symposium called "What
is a Liberal—Who is a Conservative?" in which sixty-four intellectuals
of all stripes commented on the current meaning of these political
terms and outlooks. My favorite answer was Robert Lekachman's
explanation for why he, a few years before a convinced "liberal,"
now preferred the label "radical":

> The pillars of my liberalism circa the mid-60s included moderate
> confidence in the reforming capacities of enlightened Democratic Pres-
> idents and Congresses, exaggerated attachments to Keynesian techniques
> of economic manipulation, reliance upon sustainable economic growth
> at generous rates to create enough tax revenues to finance Great Society
> programs, and faith that, none too soon, racial injustice and financial
> poverty were about to be exterminated.
>
> Why, then, a decade or so onward, do I embrace radicalism and
> bid farewell to liberalism? . . . Although much of . . . [the] fashionable
> [neo-conservative] catalogue [of criticisms of Great Society-type liberal
> reforms] impresses me as either overstated or plain wrong, . . . I concur,
> though for different reasons, in the judgement that the liberal strategies
> still in vogue are unlikely to attain their aims. I shall call radical the
> lessons I derive from recent experience. . . . [C]ontemporary (and largely
> justified) demands for group equity are too large to be satisfied at
> probable rates of future economic growth without substantial redistri-

butions of income and wealth, and such transfers can occur only in the context of serious democratic planning for sustained full employment. . . .

[I]n the 70s and later, familiar liberal objectives, notably equality of opportunity and full employment, can be approximated only after substantial structural alterations in the relation between public and private economic activity. Liberals accordingly can either trim their goals because their attainment involves changes they deplore, or they can persevere by advocating means which imply radical change. . . .

It may be that the time has come to retire honorably the word liberal and continue the debate as a dialogue between radicals and conservatives.[27]

I quite agree with Lekachman's gentle valedictory for "liberalism" as we have known it in U.S. politics since the end of the New Deal, and I would only add a couple of further thoughts in conclusion.

First, today's and tomorrow's post-liberal reformers—those committed to deepening rather than backing off from socioeconomic equity in this country—need to think and speak "radically" (in Lekachman's sense) not only about desirable new economic and social objectives for U.S. politics but also about basic governmental and party reorganizations. Planning for economic security, national industrial regeneration, and greater social equity is, for example, a fine *goal* to articulate. But it cannot be widely supported, enacted, or effectively implemented within governmental and political arrangements as they are now. Thus, effective democratic reform politics today will require (as a fully successful reformist New Deal would have required) basic changes in U.S. political arrangements.

Congressional elections and politics need to be reorganized to discourage representatives from simply brokering the established interests of the privileged and well-organized in each local constituency, and to encourage representatives instead to support sustained party programs in the interests of broad, national alliances of social groups. Political parties need to be reorganized to establish regular communication between grass-roots communities and workplace groups, on the one hand, and elected officials willing to engage in dialogue about policy proposals and policy implementation, on the other. Finally, today's conservatives are not wrong in saying that levels of governmental responsibilities in the federal system need to be reexamined and ultimately rearranged. It is just that, from a reformist perspective, reexamination should result in an *expansion* of community, regional, and national planning and in an explicit legitimation for a *broader*, rather than narrower, public sphere in U.S. capitalism and American society. And such expansion of public authority must be accompanied by an extension of political participation (in elections, at least) into the huge and growing ranks of those Americans, disproportionately less privileged, who now avoid politics altogether.

My second further thought about Lekachman's call for a new, post-liberal reformist politics is that, as a practical matter, and also in the interests of clear communication, the label "radical" will not do for those who want to continue and deepen social and political reforms in this country, rather than retreat into conservatism. "Radical" connotes for all too many Americans mindless, even violent, militancy. It brings to mind lurid images of bra-burners, street-demonstrators, and bomb-throwers. More importantly, it is silent symbolically on what reform politics should be striving *for*. "Democratic planning" and "social democracy" are less frightening and more positively evocative terms for reformist post-liberals to adopt. They are also more honest and courageous. They imply, as they should, a clear departure from previous "liberal" treatments of public action and the welfare state as merely convenient instruments for the pursuit of individualistic benefits, and they indicate a determined commitment to work steadily toward a certain kind of good society and good polity.

New Deal liberal reformers in the 1930s were stopped short of many of their best objectives, in part because they failed to work for governmental and party reorganizations from the start. Moreover, they failed to offer a sustained vision of new state actions as expressions of *public* interests and the well-being of the national *community*. By presenting the welfare state as a set of experimental instruments for the pursuit of traditional American individualist values, they left themselves and their practical liberal successors very vulnerable to constant conservative counterpressures, especially now that New Deal-style government programs do not seem to ensure or be comfortably associated with economic growth.

Now, in the 1980s, the problems faced by reformers are in many ways different from those that confronted the New Deal reformers in the 1930s. The objectives of reform politics are necessarily different in most respects today. America's economic difficulties are different, and the demands for social equity have evolved. Besides, reformers today must contend with the unintended ill-consequences of the New Deal's halfway victories. Still, present-day reformers can learn lessons from the New Deal, not by romantically harking back to its "true spirit," but by seeking to avoid analogous mistakes in political strategies. A renewed (or continued) commitment to a purely pragmatic "neo-liberalism" at this time would not only repeat the mistakes made by reformers in the 1930s. It would ensure the steady further diminution of any firm commitment to socioeconomic equity on the part of the Democratic Party, and it might facilitate the displacement of the Democrats by post-Reagan Republicans.

Robert Lekachman is right that, in one way or another, genuine political debates in America will continue not between conservatives and liberals but between conservatives and radicals, or, I would say, between conservatives and social democrats. Reformers at the cutting progressive edge of the Democratic Party, the traditional home of liberals since the 1930s, should not fear this. They should embrace it. The practical liberalism we have had since the 1940s has exhausted its distinctive contributions and visionary appeal in U.S. politics. The time has now arrived for hard political choices. And the opportunity is here to set forth a vision of American democratic politics committed to using public authority to regenerate industrial development (not just growth) and committed to ensuring economic security and cultural opportunities for *all* Americans, in bad times as well as good. This vision is not anti-capitalist. But it is social-democratic, and it definitely implies a restructuring of many aspects of existing U.S. capitalism, as well as a restructuring of our polity. Such social-democratic restructurings are going to prove necessary to get us out of our present economic and political impasse, and I, for one, see no reason why reform-minded post-liberals should not be willing to say so, loud and clear.

Notes

1. Louis Hartz, *The Liberal Tradition in America: An Interpretation of American Political Thought Since the Revolution* (New York: Harcourt, Brace, and World, 1955).

2. Ronald D. Rotunda, "The 'Liberal' Label: Roosevelt's Capture of Symbol," *Public Policy* 17 (1968):377–408. For a time, critics of the New Deal from the right insisted upon calling themselves "the true liberals." But from the late 1930s on, they accepted the label "conservative" for their position.

3. Samuel H. Beer, "Liberalism and the National Idea," in *Left, Right and Center: Essays on Liberalism and Conservatism in the United States*, edited by Robert A. Goldwin (Chicago: Rand McNally, 1965), pp. 145–46.

4. Alan Wolfe, *America's Impasse: The Rise and Fall of the Politics of Growth* (New York: Pantheon Books, 1981), especially ch. 2.

5. The Editors, "The Roosevelt Century," *The New Republic*, January 27, 1982, pp. 5–9; quotes from page 9.

6. James MacGregor Burns and Michael R. Beschloss, "The Forgotten FDR," *The New Republic*, April 7, 1982, pp. 19–22.

7. James L. Sundquist, *Dynamics of the Party System* (Washington, D.C.: The Brookings Institution, 1973), pp. 199–212; John M. Allswang, *The New Deal and American Politics* (New York: John Wiley and Sons, 1978), ch. 3; and Kristi Andersen, *The Creation of a Democratic Majority, 1928–1936* (Chicago: University of Chicago Press, 1935).

8. See especially: Richard Polenberg, *Reorganizing Roosevelt's Government, 1936–1939* (Cambridge: Harvard University Press, 1966); Richard Polenberg, "The Decline of the New Deal," in *The New Deal: The National Level*, edited by John Braeman, Robert H. Bremner, and David Brody (Columbus: Ohio State University Press, 1975); William E. Leuchtenburg, "Roosevelt, Norris and the 'Seven Little TVAs,'" *Journal of Politics* 14, no. 3 (August 1952):418–41; and James T. Patterson, *Congressional Conservatism and the New Deal* (Lexington: University of Kentucky Press, 1967), ch. 3ff.

9. David Brody, "The New Deal and World War II," in Braeman, Bremner, and Brody, eds., *The New Deal*.

10. See the full discussion in Theda Skocpol and Kenneth Finegold, "State Capacity and Economic Intervention in the Early New Deal," *The Political Science Quarterly* 97, no. 2 (Summer 1982):268–75.

11. Robert L. Tontz, "Memberships of General Farmers' Organizations, United States, 1874–1960," *Agricultural History* 38, no. 3 (July 1964):154–56; and Grant McConnell, *The Decline of Agrarian Democracy* (New York: Atheneum, 1969), ch. 7.

12. McConnell, *Agrarian Democracy*, chs. 8–10; and Sidney Baldwin, *Poverty and Politics: The Rise and Decline of the Farm Security Administration* (Chapel Hill: University of North Carolina Press, 1968). A good overview of the New Deal's agricultural programs, their political underpinnings and effects, is Richard S. Kirkendall, "The New Deal and Agriculture," in Braeman, Bremner, and Brody, eds., *The New Deal.*

13. See Patterson, *Congressional Conservatism.*

14. There are many aspects, complexly interwoven, to the story of attempts at planning and administrative rationalization in the New Deal. For overviews, see: Marion Clawson, *New Deal Planning: The National Resources Planning Board* (Baltimore and London: The Johns Hopkins University Press, 1981); Otis L. Graham, Jr., "The Planning Ideal and American Reality: The 1930s," in *The Hofstadter Aegis: A Memorial*, edited by Stanley Elkins and Eric McKitrick (New York: Alfred A. Knopf, 1974); and Barry Karl, "National Planning in the New Deal," unpublished paper, American-Soviet Conference of Historians, April 1981.

15. Polenberg, *Reorganizing Roosevelt's Government*; and Barry D. Karl, *Executive Reorganization and Reform in the New Deal* (Chicago: University of Chicago Press, 1963).

16. Some sense of this comes through in Barry D. Karl, *Charles Merriam and the Study of Politics* (Chicago: University of Chicago Press, 1974), chs.12–13.

17. A discussion of Progressive Era governmental reforms that is especially sensitive to the tensions between expertise and "efficiency," on the one hand, and politics and democracy, on the other, is Martin J. Schiesl, *The Politics of Efficiency: Municipal Administration and Reform in America: 1880–1920* (Berkeley and Los Angeles: The University of California Press, 1977).

18. *Security, Work, and Relief Policies*, Report of the Committee on Long-Range Work and Relief Policies to the National Resources Planning Board (Washington, D.C.: U.S. Government Printing Office, 1942).

19. James Holt, "The New Deal and the American Anti-Statist Tradition," in Braeman, Bremner, and Brody, eds., *The New Deal.*

20. See Stephen Skowronek, *Building a New American State* (Cambridge and New York: Cambridge University Press, 1982).

21. A good discussion of these aspects of American "political culture" appears in Ira Katznelson and Kenneth Prewitt, "Constitutionalism, Class, and the Limits of Choice in U.S. Foreign Policy," in *Capitalism and the State in U.S.-Latin American Relations*, edited by Richard R. Fagen (Stanford, Cal.: Stanford University Press, 1979), pp. 27–33.

22. *The Chicago Tribune*, Wednesday, February 17, 1982, pp. 1,4. All quotes are from the article.

23. Michael Walzer, "The Community," *The New Republic*, March 31, 1982, pp. 11-14.

24. "The Agenda After Reagan" (a set of seven articles), *The New Republic*, March 31, 1982, pp. 11–33.

25. Lester Thurow, "The Economy," *The New Republic*, March 31, 1982, pp. 24–25.

26. Walzer, "The Community," pp. 11 (quote) and 14.

27. *Commentary* 62 no. 3 (September 1976):76–77.

7

Liberalism in Retreat

CHRISTOPHER LASCH

In theory, the liberal order should have collapsed a long time ago. Its lack of a public philosophy; its inability to base any theory of justice on the common needs of the community; the incompatible claims that can be founded on an appeal to the interests of the individual (the only basis of social policy liberalism acknowledges)— these deficiencies make it impossible for liberalism to articulate a theory of the good society or to reconcile the claims of competing interest groups. In practice, however, liberal states have been spared the worst consequences of their internal incoherence by repeated, prolonged periods of economic expansion. An abundance of economic resources has made it possible to satisfy two incompatible sets of demands—those based on property and those based on considerations of equality; or if not to satisfy them, at least to prevent the conflict between them from erupting into a full-scale social explosion.

The claim that property-holders are entitled to enjoy the fruits of their enterprise with a minimum of interference from the state obviously conflicts with the claim that the state has an obligation to provide the less fortunate members of society, in John Rawls's words, with "liberty and opportunity, income and wealth, . . . the bases of self-respect"—in other words, to assure an equitable distribution of "primary goods."[1] But when the state can finance a relative redistribution of wealth out of an expanding pool of resources so that nobody suffers an absolute decline in his standard of living, the aggrieved property-holder will content himself with rhetorical denunciations of bleeding-heart liberals and big spenders without mounting a frontal assault on policies that he may even perceive, moreover— however dimly—as a necessary contribution to social peace. Thus during World War II, at the height of the liberal era, the American government achieved a modest redistribution of income in a climate of rapid economic growth, not by setting a limit on earnings but by the simple expedient of allowing "the rich to get richer at a somewhat slower rate than it allowed the poor to get richer."[2] As a result, the "share of national income held by the richest 5% of the people declined from 23.7% to 16.8%," while the number of families with incomes under $2,000 fell by more than half. The political compromises available in a more expansive era are most vividly conveyed by the statistic that the poorest fifth increased its income by 68 percent between 1941 and 1945, while the income of the upper fifth increased by only 20 percent.[3] This was the last time in American history, by the way, that any significant redistribution of income was achieved; but it was achieved, in those happier days, without lowering the income of any sector of the population.

Those who insist that American liberal democracy has always rested on the frontier, on an expanding area of free land and more generally on economic expansion, have grasped something of central importance, even if they have confused the argument with a lyrical celebration of pioneer virtues or with the dubious contention that the frontier served literally as a safety valve by draining off discontented workers from the East. The point is that economic expansion helped to smooth over the underlying conflicts of a liberal society, between individual liberty and social justice, property and equality. After the official closing of the frontier in 1890, liberals repeatedly had to face the possibility that a day of reckoning might be approaching in which the contradictions at the heart of liberal democracy could no longer be evaded. During the progressive period, uneasiness over the closing of the frontier helped to precipitate discussions about the concentration of wealth and the growth of poverty and class conflict on a scale that threatened to tear society apart. Wartime expansion, followed by the boom times of the twenties, temporarily put an end to those discussions, but they surfaced again during the Depression, just as they had surfaced during the hard times of the 1890s, when people first began to fear that the age of expansion had come to an end. The same fear was a prominent theme in the thought and practice of the early New Deal.

In his famous speech at the Commonwealth Club in San Francisco during the presidential campaign of 1932, Franklin D. Roosevelt announced that the country had long ago reached its "last frontier."[4] The "safety valve," he went on to argue, had disappeared. "Our industrial plant is built" and possibly "overbuilt." These developments, according to Roosevelt, called for a "reappraisal of values." Formerly society had chosen "to give the ambitious man free play" only because the availability of free land, the rapid growth of population, and the inadequacy of the existing plant made the industrialist a social benefactor in spite of himself. In a "closer economic system," Roosevelt appeared to say, government would have to take a more active part in bringing about a more equitable distribution of wealth and resources. In the language of later disputes (say, the dispute between John

Rawls and Robert Nozick), claims based on entitlement would have to give way to claims based on need.

Unfortunately the "reappraisal of values" Roosevelt called for fell short of a reexamination of the central premises of liberalism itself. No one proved more reluctant to reconsider fundamental issues than Roosevelt himself. Indeed he went on to assure his audience at the Commonwealth Club (an audience made up of wealthy industrialists, after all) that nothing he had just said should be construed as an attack on the business corporation as an institution. He may have deplored the social irresponsibility of the "princes of property," as he called them (even this sounds like pretty strong language by the mild standards of our own time) but he cautioned against any inclination to "abandon the principle of the strong economic units called corporations, merely because their power is susceptible of easy abuse." The Commonwealth Club speech called not so much for social justice as for "enlightened administration."

Enlightened administration in the form of the NRA failed, of course, to save the day, and after the collapse of the NRA, an older argument about the concentration of power and the inevitability of large-scale organization, an argument begun in 1912, started up again and divided the New Dealers into rival factions, each with its own solution of the trust question, as the progressives had called it. Some wanted national economic planning. Others welcomed large-scale organization in industry and private economic planning, euphemistically known as "self-government in industry," but opposed planning by the state. Another group of advisers accepted the inevitability of corporations but proposed to encourage counterorganization among workers, farmers, and consumers in order to set practical limits to corporate power. Another faction pointed out that a liberal use of the spending power would stabilize economic conditions without any need for structural reforms at all. Still another faction sought to restore economic competition through anti-trust prosecutions and legislation against monopolies. Even the trust-busters, however, with a few exceptions proposed only to enforce competition, not to set limits on size. They too, most of them, took for granted the technical advantages of large-scale organization.

All in all, New Deal debates about the problem of monopoly, as Ellis Hawley has shown, suggest that the New Dealers, like the American people as a whole, wanted the best of both worlds. They wanted the material benefits of modern organization without sacrificing the values of individualism and democracy.[5] Given these contradictory objectives, it is hardly surprising that they failed to solve the problem.

In the end, none of the various strategies for reform that gained a hearing in the thirties achieved a decisive victory over the others. Instead of adopting a coherent line of policy, the Roosevelt administration, followed in this respect by subsequent liberal regimes, flitted from one strategy to another and committed itself firmly to none. Having failed to come to grips with the central problem of American society, the concentration of economic power, and having failed to choose among competing solutions, liberals condemned themselves to a series of improvisations intended to satisfy various claimant groups and constituencies but having no broader objective than to keep the peace and to avoid confrontations that might have to be settled by invoking the coercive powers of the state. The resulting system of interest-group politics, the system that came into being in the thirties, dominated the politics of the next forty years, and is now falling apart, has been variously characterized as a system of countervailing power, as a form of pluralism, and as "political capitalism." These labels are misleading in various ways, but each captures an important feature of the advanced liberal state.

Instead of curbing the power of corporations, liberal administrations since the thirties have hoped that other organized interests, with a little help from the state, would somehow hold the corporations in check. They have used theories of pluralism as a rationale for their own indecisiveness. Yet it is increasingly clear that the distribution of power in the United States is not really pluralistic, since representation in decisionmaking tends to be confined to spokesmen for the dominant interest groups. Among those groups, moreover, corporations continue to exercise the lion's share of political and economic power.

On the other hand, the concept of political capitalism, which recognizes that the expansion of state power has benefited corporations more than anyone else, is misleading in its own right if it means that business interests engineered this expansion of the state or that the state merely carries out their bidding. Businessmen tend to judge policies almost entirely by their immediate impact on the market, particularly on the climate for investment, whereas the liberal state, even if it serves the interests of capital in the long run, has had to undertake an extensive array of programs (often in the face of business opposition) designed to benefit other groups, to co-opt political dissidence, to head off demands for more radical change, and to bring about some measure of social justice in a country still based ostensibly at least on egalitarian principles.

The growth of the welfare functions of the state and of social services in general has greatly enlarged the influence and the sheer size of those classes or social strata engaged not in the production of goods but in the maintenance of the capitalist system as a whole. These professional and managerial strata have developed interests of their own and a point of view that often conflicts with the immediate interests of corporate capital. One does not have to accept either the idea of a managerial revolution or the pluralist theory of "veto groups" and "countervailing power" to see that a small class of rich property owners no longer controls American business and politics or acts as a ruling class in the accepted sense of the term. One does not have to accept the contention that the old capitalist class has been displaced by a new oligarchy of administrators, managers, and bureaucrats to see the general validity of David Riesman's observation that "explicit class leadership" died with McKinley.[6]

The general crisis of authority is the most obvious sign of its obsolescence: the exhaustion of ruling-class ideologies, the inability of elites to provide a coherent justification of their own power, the retreat from arguments about principles, the resort to psychological manipulation in place of ideological coercion. The new therapeutic, permissive styles of leadership, now under renewed attack from the right, dispense with appeals to authority, side sentimentally with the underdog and the outcast, and seek to co-opt dissension through programs of affirmative action and "innovative" social change. That such programs leave the existing distribution of wealth unchanged does not establish the existence of a ruling class in any important sense of the term. Even proponents of a ruling-class theory of American society admit that we cannot "infer power from the distribution of wealth, income, health, education, and other benefits."[7]

The New Deal may have backed away from a confrontation with corporate power, and its reform programs may have proved incoherent and inconclusive, but these programs did have the effect of committing the liberal state to the cause of the underprivileged. Indeed these commitments followed more or less directly from the failure to challenge corporate power. Failing to scale down this power or to restore competitive conditions (if these were ever real possibilities), liberals had no hope of stabilizing the economy and reviving people's confidence in the future except to spend lavishly on social services, to promote mass consumption, and to make it easier for disadvantaged groups to organize in their own self-defense. Their only hope of keeping social peace, in other words, lay in policies designed to appease dissident groups and to improve their competitive position in the marketplace.

In the expansive economic conditions of the forties, fifties, and sixties, the most sustained period of economic growth in the country's history, strategies of co-optation proved remarkably successful. In the long run, however, they have driven the state to the verge of bankruptcy and alienated most of the constituency that kept liberal governments in power during the long period of Democratic Party ascendancy. Spending on social services rose steadily throughout the period of liberal rule, especially during the sixties with the establishment of the poverty program, the broadening of the Social Security system, increased aid to education, the adoption of the Medicare program, and so on.

When combined with lavish expenditures on highway construction and especially on defense, the growth of federal spending placed a heavy burden on the taxpayers and for the most part on the very taxpayers who could least afford to bear it, or in any case enjoyed the fewest measurable benefits from this spending. The working class and the lower middle class have been taxed to support programs that benefited the poor and the rich. Elementary considerations of fairness would require that corporations bear most of the cost of supporting the federal government, since it serves their interests in so many ways: by providing social insurance against political unrest; by providing a system of indirect subsidies to business whereby the state assumes some of the secondary costs of production, such as personnel training, research, and development; and by providing a foreign policy, backed up by massive military forces, that has the object (among others) of stabilizing political conditions throughout the world and maintaining a favorable climate for foreign investments.

Instead of bearing their share of the cost of supporting the state, however, the corporations have managed to shift the burden to working people already suffering from inflation, while convincing them that most of their taxes go not to support American corporate enterprise but to support an army of welfare chiselers and pointy-headed government bureaucrats who make careers out of minding other people's business. Every level of government, state, local, and national, rests on highly regressive forms of taxation. Thus whereas at the beginning of the century, property taxes raised over 80 percent of all state and local revenues, today they account for only half of local budgets and a mere 5 percent of state budgets. Sales and income taxes make up most of the difference, and in spite of appearances, state and federal income tax laws discriminate against lower-income groups.

> According to available studies, the average rate of taxation on the highest incomes is roughly 30 per cent, chiefly because of the special treatment granted to capital gains income, deductions (mainly applicable to those who receive relatively high incomes), and income splitting and exemptions (which benefit high income families relatively more than low income groups). In point of fact, no one apart from independent professionals and small and middle businessmen pays more than a 25 per cent rate because of the ease of short-circuiting income into non-taxable forms (e.g., expense accounts) and of tax evasion which is most widespread among farmers and those who receive interest income and annuities.[8]

Income taxes and sales taxes do not begin to exhaust the list of devices by which the propertied classes shift the tax burden to the poor. In union negotiations, employers until recently have preferred wage increases to benefits; wage increases, which can be passed on to the consumer, take the form of taxable income. The prolongation of the age of retirement serves the same purpose by converting benefits into taxable income.

The mounting tax burden on lower middle-income families is only a small part of the story—the story, that is, of the decline of the liberal coalition. Another part of the story is inflation, which has to be seen (in part) as another by-product of government spending that falls once again with special force on the so-called middle classes—that is, on operatives, clerks, the lower ranks of sales personnel, municipal workers, schoolteachers, and small proprietors. Then there is the Vietnam war, which not only initiated the present trend of acute inflation but further widened the rift between "middle America," as it has come to call itself, and the Democratic Party.

Here again the misnamed middle class bore the burden of policies it had no share in making, since college students enjoyed exemption from the draft while many lower-class youth, on the other hand, failed to qualify for it. The working classes thus came to hate both the war and the anti-war movement led by upper middle-class students who flaunted their privileged status even on those rare occasions when they called (in the accents of an alien political tradition) for a revolutionary alliance of students and workers.

Issues like crime, "law and order," and busing, which have been manipulated by the right ever since the late sixties, when Nixon rode them to the White House, spring from the same inequity in the distribution of the costs of liberal reform. The urban working class has paid the price for the decay of industrial cities, the impoverishment of municipal governments, and the racial integration of public education by means of busing. Government policy ever since the forties has tended in all sorts of ways to encourage the abandonment of the city by the affluent at the same time that the welfare system has had to expand in order to take care of the poverty-stricken people left behind. The working classes find themselves caught in the middle again—a forgotten majority in a society characterized by vast extremes of poverty and wealth. In the sixties, battles over racial policy and poverty programs in New York, in which the Lindsay regime appeared to draw its chief support from an alliance of organized philanthropy and the ghetto poor—of black power and the Ford Foundation—provided one of the first demonstrations of the new alignments that were shattering the old Roosevelt coalition.

Still we have only begun to scratch the surface. One of the effects of liberal policy, as Walter Dean Burnham has pointed out, is to raise the cost of social services—medical services, for example—that have to be purchased on the open market, while providing them at reduced cost to poor people. "The working lower middle classes," Burnham notes, "again and again found themselves in a situation in which they could not afford to purchase goods in the private market . . .

which were provided—after a fashion, no doubt—to those who could pass the means test required. . . . They always seemed to make just enough . . . not to qualify for public help, while not enough to get what they needed through the market sector."9

Burnham and other observers have called attention to another feature of liberal social policy that alienates the working classes, once the mainstay of the liberal movements—its growing reliance on the courts and on bureaucratic agencies to achieve its purposes. The Supreme Court, wisely or foolishly, thrust itself into the vanguard of social reform with its decisions on school integration, reapportionment, and abortion, and the result of judicial activism has been to encourage every claimant group to take its case first of all to the courts. Women, blacks, the elderly, Mexican Americans, homosexuals, single parents, advocates of "alternative life-styles" all perceive, quite correctly, that the ends they seek are unpopular with the masses of voters. Judicial reform, especially now that it has been sanctified by its part in the struggle against racial segregation in the South, which might otherwise still be in existence, appears to be the most effective way to circumvent public inertia or opposition. When the courts respond favorably to such appeals, however, their decisions have the effect, not merely of emphasizing the unpopularity of the causes in question, but of creating new bureaucracies charged with responsibility for enforcing the courts' guidelines for social reform. The "proliferation of claimant groups," their growing recourse to insider strategies, and the bureaucratic structures to which those strategies lead have contributed enormously to the alienation of masses of voters from the Democratic Party. The strategy of bureaucratic reform "has worked across time to undermine the legitimacy of the party. . . . The politics of a country founded very importantly upon [public] opinion cannot indefinitely be supported without it, and still less in its teeth."10

The bureaucratic method of reform has come to rely heavily not merely on the courts but on the mass media, another legacy of the civil rights movement, which first revealed the power of those media, especially television, to dramatize social injustices. "Before television," an NBC correspondent has written, "the American public had no idea of the abuses blacks suffered in the South. We showed them what was happening; the brutality, the police dogs, the miserable conditions. . . . We made it impossible for Congress not to act."11 By dramatizing the poverty of Appalachia, the media played a similar part in the genesis of the anti-poverty program. Their role in stimulating opposition to the war in Vietnam is well known. It is no wonder that control of the media by the "Eastern liberal establishment" became another rallying-cry in the Nixon-Agnew campaign. The truth behind this misconceived formula was that liberal politics had become to a large extent a politics of the mass media, not merely because the media tended, inadvertently rather than by design, to create support for liberal policies, but because they so often seemed to reflect liberal values and a growing liberal condescension toward the values of "middle America."

The upwardly mobile managerial and professional elites with which latter-day liberalism is so closely associated, having turned their backs on the ethnic ghettos from which so many of them originally sprang, and having developed a cosmopolitan outlook and cosmopolitan tastes through higher education (and through reading *Cosmopolitan*), now look back on their origins with a mixture of superiority and sentimental regret. Their ideology of tolerance and anti-authoritarianism puts great emphasis on the ability to outgrow early prejudices. Because the new class has defined itself in opposition to the values of "middle America," it needs to repudiate its own roots, to exaggerate the distance it has traveled, and also to exaggerate the racism and bigotry of those lower down on the social scale. At the same time, it occasionally sheds a sentimental tear over the simpler life it thinks it has left behind. Prone to bouts of nostalgia, it assumes that anyone who uses the past as a standard against which to measure the present shares this nostalgia and the hang-ups about the past with which it is associated.

All these attitudes find almost classic expression in Norman Lear's comedy of popular ignorance and parochialism, *All in the Family*, continued in the series *Archie Bunker's Place*. Central documents in the cultural civil war that now divides America, these series tell us a great deal (one is tempted to say they tell us just about all we need to know) not of course about the mind of middle America, but about the contemporary liberal mind and the alienation of liberalism from its constituency.

When *All in the Family* first appeared, in 1971, an older generation of liberals denounced it on the grounds that it sanitized prejudice and made it socially acceptable. Liberals like Laura Hobson, convinced that bigotry can be combatted only by propaganda depicting it in the most unattractive light, mistakenly saw the Archie Bunker programs as a capitulation to popular prejudice. What the programs really seem to say, however, is that prejudice is a disease and that the only way to overcome it, as in psychotherapy, is to bring to light its irrational origins. *All in the Family* "simply airs [prejudice]," according to Lear, "brings it out in the open, has people talking about it." The programs implicitly take the position that resistance to social change, failure to "adjust" to change, and fear of change have pathological roots. Lear has argued that Archie Bunker's bigotry rests not on hatred but on the "fear of anything he doesn't understand."[12] Because this fear is irrational, Archie's prejudices cannot be corrected by rational persuasion.

Both these series seem to have been influenced, at least indirectly, by the theory of "working-class authoritarianism," which has played an important part in the thinking of social scientists and members of the helping professions ever since the late forties. According to this widely accepted interpretation, prejudice, ethnocentricity, and intolerance of ambiguity originate in the authoritarian childrearing practices allegedly characteristic of working-class families. Archie Bunker has all the traits commonly attributed to the authoritarian husband and father. Lear's dramatization of Bunker's anti-Semitism, racism, male chauvinism, and xenophobia shares with the sociological literature on authoritarianism a tendency to reinterpret class issues in therapeutic terms and to reduce political conflicts to psychological ones. It ignores the possibility that "middle Americans" have legitimate grievances against society, legitimate misgivings about what is called social progress.

Yet the gains that have been made in race relations, desegregation, and women's rights—gains, it should be stressed again, that are enjoyed principally by members of the managerial and professional classes—have usually been achieved at the expense of the white working class, particularly the white working-class male. His anger cannot be understood, therefore, as a purely psychological reaction; it has an important political basis. His dislike of liberals, moreover, springs not so much from "anti-intellectualism" or ethnocentricity as from the realistic perception that working-class values are the chief casualties of the "cultural revolution" with which liberalism has increasingly identified itself (for example, at the 1972 convention of the Democratic Party). With his unsentimental but firm commitment to marriage and family life, his respect for hard work and individual enterprise, and his admittedly old-fashioned belief that people should accept the consequences of their actions, the working-class male rightly regards himself as a forgotten man in a society increasingly dominated by the permissive, therapeutic morality of universal understanding. He sees himself, not without reason, as the victim of bureaucratic interference, welfarism, and sophisticated ridicule.

Deserted by the left and by the opinion-makers and policy-makers, lacking any real choices, clinging to a culture that is widely regarded as backward and authoritarian, the "middle American" has become increasingly defensive and even reactionary in his outlook, thereby fulfilling the expectations of the intelligentsia and confirming their prejudices. The politics of personal liberation and therapeutic enlightenment have divided liberals from the common people (as they used to be called)—from people who reject the permissive morality of self-actualization not because it offends their "petty bourgeois sensibilities," as liberals like to think, but because it offends their sense of reality. A therapeutic morality that demands sympathy and understanding for criminals, sex offenders, and juvenile delinquents offends popular ideas of justice, according to which people should accept responsibility for the choices they make. The campaign for legalized abortion stirs up the same feelings. Feminism impressed working class men, and working class women too, for that matter, as a movement dominated by professional women and indifferent to the harsher conditions experienced by the masses. The well-publicized campaign against the nuclear family, conducted not only by feminists but by middle-class radicals, the helping professions, and other spokesmen for progressive points of view, has little attraction to people who have no illusions about marriage and family life, yet recognize that domestic responsibilities represent a stabilizing influence, a source of personal discipline, in a world where personal disintegration remains always an imminent danger.

It took the Reagan revolution to awaken liberals to the erosion of their working-class constituency and to the depth of the disaffection with liberalism that now prevails. But the reaction to these events does not encourage a belief in the resilience or vitality of the liberal tradition. The reaction can be summed up as a mixture of incredulity, hysteria, and the kind of soul-searching that nevertheless exempts the most important premises from reconsideration.

Some liberals continue to deny that Reaganism reflects a fundamental change in American politics; these wishful thinkers may be due for further disappointments. Some have merely intensified their propaganda on behalf of abortion, gay rights, and the Equal Rights Amendment. Others have begun to talk about the need to reappropriate the defense of family values and to counter right-wing manipulation of cultural issues. This is much the most promising reaction; but the idea that the right has manipulated issues like the family implies that these are not real issues at all. On this view the important issues are economic, not cultural, and the left can best recover from recent defeats by reviving the good old issues of employment, poverty, medical care, and equal access to education.

The trouble with this program is that economic issues and cultural issues are intertwined, now as in the past. The same people who resent the erosion of their standard of living by the deadly combination of inflation and economic contraction also resent liberal attacks on their values. They want more than a decent livelihood, they want some acknowledgment of the legitimacy of their commitment to marriage, their patriotism, their religion, and their belief that the differences between men and women cannot be reduced to cultural "conditioning" and economic oppression.

If liberals were more confident of their own values, they might see that it is possible to raise these questions without demanding a return to the dark ages, to value patriotism, say, without unleashing a wave of xenophobia, or to imagine a nonsexist division of labor between the sexes. But the ascendancy of the new class rests not on its secure command of an intellectual and political tradition, but on its imagined superiority to the average unenlightened American bigot.

In any case its outlook and interests are closely bound up with the rise of the modern corporation, and liberals are not likely, therefore, to embark on a reconsideration of their political faith that would lead them to question among other things their belief in the desirability of continual change or lead them, indeed, to the conclusion that the corporation itself is the most important source not just of inequality and injustice, but of the mania for change, formerly known as progress, that has made our society such a nightmare.

Notes

1. John Rawls, *A Theory of Justice* (Cambridge: Harvard University Press, 1971), p. 303.

2. Richard Polenberg, *One Nation Divisible: Class, Race, and Ethnicity in the United States since 1938* (New York: Viking Press, 1980), p. 62.

3. Ibid., p. 64.

4. Basil Rauch, ed., *Selected Speeches, Messages, Press Conferences, and Letters of Franklin D. Roosevelt* (New York: Rinehart, 1957), pp. 74–85.

5. Ellis Hawley, *The New Deal and the Problem of Monopoly* (Princeton: Princeton University Press, 1966), pp. 315, 402, 472–73.

6. David Riesman, *The Lonely Crowd* (New Haven: Yale University Press, 1950), p. 237.

7. G. William Domhoff, *The Powers That Be: Processes of Ruling-Class Domination in America* (New York: Random House, 1978), p. 9.

8. James O'Connor, "The Fiscal Crisis of the State," pt. II, *Socialist Revolution*, vol. 1 (1970), pp. 72–73.

9. Walter Dean Burnham, "The Reagan Revolution and the Eclipse of the Democratic Party," pt. II, p. 12, unpublished paper presented to a meeting of the editorial board of *democracy*, September, 1981. A greatly abridged version of this paper appeared in *democracy*, vol. 2 (July, 1982), pp. 7–17.

10. Burnham, "The Reagan Revolution," pt. II, p. 12.

11. Quoted in Polenberg, *One Nation Divisible*, p. 184.

12. Richard P. Adler, ed., *All in the Family: A Critical Appraisal* (New York: Praeger, 1979), p. 107.

8

Liberalism and Two Conceptions of the State

MICHAEL WILLIAMS

Liberals like to think of themselves as moderates. But to liberalism's detractors, liberal moderation seems less a virtue than the reflection of theoretical incoherence, failure of nerve, or both.

From the left, the complaint is that liberal reform never goes far enough. Liberals try to soften the harshest effects produced by our economic, political, and social institutions but either fail to appreciate or lack the will to tackle their underlying causes. So while the liberal's concern with social welfare, the advancement of minorities, the regulation of the workplace, and so on points to his sharing many goals with the democratic socialist, a lingering and excessive regard for the market, or for established institutions generally, makes him half-hearted and ineffective in their pursuit. It is as if the liberal wills the end but shrinks from willing the means. Various ways of accounting for this suggest themselves, few flattering.

There is a complementary complaint from the right. To the conservative, the liberal's regard for individual rights, personal freedom, and the rule of law suggests that he ought to be an ally in the defense of liberty to which collectivism in its various guises is seen as the greatest threat. But again, the liberal is apt to seem a disappointingly weak-kneed ally. The humanitarian urge to improve everyone's lot, often perceived as a quest for "social justice," while commendable enough in its way, has all too frequently been sadly ill-thought-through. Assisted no doubt by the need to placate the interest groups that compose liberalism's constituency, it has pushed liberals even further in the direction of collectivist and paternalist policies to the extent that out of a misguided urge to impose universal well-being, liberalism threatens to undermine the economic, social, and political institutions on which our liberty and ultimately even our welfare depend. So again, liberalism is seen to embody confusion of mind compounded by failure of nerve.

The confusion of mind consists, specifically, in the liberal's reluctance to acknowledge the true basis of our freedom. For the conservative, freedom can exist only in a society that respects a clear distinction between the public and private spheres and recognizes clear limits to the extent that government may legitimately interfere with the lives of the governed. But the foundation of the private sphere is private property, an institution toward which the liberal penchant for interventionist economic policies encourages far too cavalier an attitude. Correlatively, the liberal's taste for social reform has worked to undermine the traditional values associated with family, home, and neighborhood, exacerbating social problems, which will then be argued to call for yet more government action. In their reckless desire to advance the cause of what they consider to be progress, liberals are likely to succeed only in extending ever further the intrusive power of the state.

Obviously, the complaints from left and right share considerable common ground. Socialists and conservatives would both like to see liberals decide where their deepest loyalties lie. Difficult economic conditions, springing from deep causes and admitting no easy solutions, make the liberal attempt to be all things to all people an exercise in either foolishness or self-deception.

Now, it seems to me that, though its basic tendency stamps it as criticism from the left, Professor Lasch's attack on liberalism also involves significant elements from the conservative's battery of complaints.[1] (In this respect it is reminiscent of some of Orwell's social criticism.) So examining his argument should be more than an exercise in *ad hominem* refutation: it should provide an occasion for reflecting on what might be said in favor of liberalism. But I want to come at this by first reconstructing Lasch's argument in my own way. To do this I need to make a distinction that informs Lasch's discussion but is never explicitly drawn. Lasch uses "liberal" in two senses. When opposed to "conservative," "liberal" indicates a certain kind of "progressive" attitude toward public policy—in practical terms, a willingness to see the government, particularly the federal government, take on a larger role in securing the well-being of the governed. But when it occurs in his phrase "the liberal order," "liberal" points not toward a proclivity for certain kinds of policies but toward a more general conception of political life and the institutions of government. To avoid confusion, I shall speak of "liberal progressivism" when I want to contrast liberalism with conservatism, reserving "Liberalism" (capital "L") for the general conception of political life that informs the Liberal order.

How are we to understand Liberalism and the Liberal political order? As we shall see, Lasch favors identifying Liberalism in theoretical terms—Liberalism is founded on the attempt to make private interest the foundation of public life. But I think it is better to begin by identifying the Liberal order in more concrete terms as the form of political life most clearly exemplified by the United States, Western Europe, and the English-speaking commonwealth countries. Of course, there are notable differences between members of this group. But all display certain typical institutions: representative multiparty government elected by popular franchise, independent judiciary, free press, extensive civil liberties, a large private economic sector, and so on.

This should serve as a preliminary identification of what I mean by "Liberalism" and "the Liberal order." If we seek a deeper understanding, it had best be historical. Liberalism emerged as the modern state emerged, in response to a perceived danger. States in the modern sense grew out of the confusion of medieval Europe and brought to light a new and potentially threatening form of political authority. The emergence of a modern state necessarily involved eliminating all kinds of traditional liberties and privileges. Local systems of law had to be incorporated into a national system or else abolished; the powers of the Church co-opted or extinguished; and semi-independent municipalities, fiefdoms, and so on brought firmly under central control. These developments mark the emergence of the "sovereign" state, of government subject to no higher competing or external authority, empowered to make and amend laws as it sees fit. Classical Liberalism developed as a doctrine aimed at ensuring that this new kind of authority, armed with an increasingly effective apparatus of government, did not become the basis of the worst kind of tyranny. Hence Liberalism is a doctrine of rights, but in the first instance rights *against* the government—rights of property, free speech, assembly, and so on, all of which, once recognized, provide a bulwark against the usurpation of all aspects of life by the political authorities.

The advantage of identifying Liberalism and the Liberal order in concrete, historical terms is that doing so allows us to fix what we are talking about without prejudging the issue of what unifying theoretical conception underlies the Liberal polity or even if there is one. It may be that we should think of the Liberal order generally as de Tocqueville thought of the American democracy, as patched together from institutions and devices reflecting diverse and even contrary political tendencies, though not necessarily the worse for that. (As Burke reminds us, politics is not geometry.) Furthermore, although the theoretical considerations cited to justify various forms of political life often prove less than overwhelmingly convincing, the lack of a convincing theoretical justification does not deprive a particular form of life of all its real virtues. So, if we insist on beginning with a theoretical identification of the Liberal order, not only is there the obvious danger of misidentifying its theoretical basis, but there is also the possibility of persuading ourselves that we have found a fatal weakness in a concrete form of life when all we have done is to report flaws in an attempt to provide it with a theoretical foundation. Lasch falls into both traps.

Lasch's fundamental thesis is that the Liberal order should have collapsed long ago. This is because Liberalism, understood as the theory informing the Liberal order, is hopelessly inadequate as a basis for a stable and satisfying form of political and social life. Its central flaw, which is also its essence, lies in its attempt to make self-interest the mainspring of our social existence. The appeal to individual interest serves both to generate incompatible claims and to preclude the articulation of a "public philosophy," a theory of justice based on "the common needs of the community," which alone would provide for their adjudication.[2]

Translating theoretical deficiencies into concrete, historical terms, we see that it is the fate of the Liberal political order, by tolerating or even encouraging vast extremes of wealth and poverty, to generate social tensions that threaten to tear it apart. This is where liberal progressivism comes in. Its mild reformism tries to reduce the pressure by interpolating into the Liberal political order elements of a welfare state. But it is crucial to recognize that liberal progressivism, as much as conservatism (in America, anyway, where conservatism is not linked to reactionary-aristocratic politics), is a tendency *within* the Liberal order and so constrained by it. Liberal progressivism's commitment to Liberalism prevents it from undertaking any truly fundamental reform; the structure of wealth and privilege that has evolved within the Liberal order will never be attacked as such. Accordingly, as Lasch sees it, liberal progressivism is condemned to a hand-to-mouth existence, patching up here and there, buying off whatever claimant groups are most powerful, most vocal, or best organized (which need not be the most deserving or, indeed, deserving at all).

This is not to say that liberal progressivism has achieved nothing, for it has evidently sponsored significant reform. The point is rather that the economic and social costs of its achievements have not been equitably distributed. It is not much of an exaggeration to say that Lasch sees liberal progressivism as a conspiracy of the rich and poor against the working and middle class majority, the rich guarding their privileges and the poor increasing their benefits.

As long as the economy continued to expand, claimant groups could be appeased and social-welfare programs funded without anyone's really noticing who was paying. However, a contracting economy, an increasingly punitive tax burden (reflecting a tax system in which shelters and loopholes mostly benefit the better-off), and runaway inflation put an end to all this and paved the way for the breakup of the electoral coalition on which liberal progressivism's political ascendancy was founded.

Add to this the inequitable distribution of the social costs of liberal progressive reform. Court-ordered busing to achieve integration, for example, has tended to have its greatest impact on working-class neighborhoods. We may speculate that economic and social discontents magnify one another, for in times of economic uncertainty, the security and support provided by family, neighborhood, and church, though rooted in a nexus of loyalties and values that enlightened opinion is apt to look askance at, become even more important.

These reflections bring us to what Lasch sees as another dimension of the failure of liberal progressivism: the widening cultural gap between liberal opinion leaders and their one-time electoral constituency. Having escaped or never experienced the realities of ordinary working life, they are inclined to despise "traditional" values connected with work, family, and individual responsibility. Moreover, this condescending attitude tempts liberal progressives to account for resistance to their policies in terms of prejudice, authoritarianism, and other forms of irrationality. This therapeutic attitude toward the dissenter is less tolerant than it is sometimes made to seem. It tolerates him by reducing his speech to cognitive insignificance, treating his utterances as symptoms rather than political judgments. This is the self-deceiving strategy by which liberal progressives are tempted to mask the political shortcomings of liberal progressivism.

So much for my reconstruction of Professor Lasch's diagnosis. As for his remedy, I am less certain, but it seems to be something like this. Conservatives hold that the way out of our troubles must involve a return to first principles, from which liberal progressive reforms are seen as a dereliction. Since it was the inadequacy and incoherence of those principles that generated liberal progressivism in the first place, this will not do. Nevertheless, we must take conservative criticism seriously and not try to explain it away, as liberal progressives are apt to do. We must take it as pointing to the inadequacy of Liberalism, not just, as conservatives think, of liberal progressivism. If there is a cure for our political and economic ills, it will emerge only through our making the Liberal order the object of a radical critique that liberal progressivism, because of its own theoretical ties to Liberalism, has been unable to undertake.

This picture of liberal progressivism is unflattering and, I suspect, not entirely fair. It is hard to believe that the liberal coalition could have lasted so long if the majority of ordinary Americans had not been the beneficiaries of liberal progressive policies, not just a convenient source of revenue. (Think of Social Security, cheap mortgages, student loan programs, etc.) But the details are not really what I want to argue about. To come to terms with this attack on "liberalism" we must add to our understanding of the Liberal order.

The Liberal order is one form of the modern state. Though the roots of some characteristic Liberal institutions may be traced back to the Middle Ages, medieval realms are not Liberal states. We may be able to get some insight into Liberalism, then, by asking some more general questions about the modern state. What is a *state*? Obviously, some kind of association of human beings. But what kind of association? How are persons associated when they are members of a single state?

In a profound and important essay, the British political philosopher Michael Oakeshott suggests that the modern state emerged as and has remained an inherently ambiguous undertaking.[3] Theorists of the late Middle Ages, he argues, recognized two fundamental forms of human association, which they identified by terms taken from Roman law, *societas* and *universitas*. In Oakeshott's view, the two modes of association thus identified have recurrently suggested themselves both as paradigms in terms of which the modern state might be understood and ideals in the light of which it might be shaped. States as they emerged and have evolved have always offered intimations of both forms of association; nor on the level of ideals has one conception of the state ever won a complete victory over the other. It may be that these two forms of human association correspond to deep and divergent human aspirations.

A *societas* is what may be called a *formal* association. Human agents are associated in this way when they jointly recognize the authority of a system of rules governing conduct. These rules, however, will not determine what the agents are to do, in the sense of what goals to pursue or what interests to promote. Rather they will specify a code of conduct—limitations to be respected in the pursuit of any goals, individual or communal, whatever they might be. In the Middle Ages, the human race was often thought to constitute a *societas*. It could not be supposed that all mankind was involved in some common project (what could it be?). But in their dealings with each other, all were subject to the law of nature, established by God to regulate the pursuit of their various contingent projects. Or we might think of the speakers of a common language as associated in this formal way. In speaking a language we subscribe to rules governing how sentences are to be put together; we agree on *how* things are to be said; but this is not at all an agreement to say anything in particular, still less to say the same things.

It is worth emphasizing that, in an important sense, association in a *societas* is a form of moral relationship. A moral community exists when agents are bound by mutual recognition of prescriptions regulating how their particular goals, desires, and interests may be pursued and satisfied. As Kant stresses perhaps more than any other modern moral theorist, a moral relationship is not constituted by a pact to pursue some particular contingent goal, nor is such a relationship dissolved by the achievement of some particular satisfaction. If we de-emphasize Kant's tendency to think that the categorical imperative suffices for the deduction of specific duties, we can think of his notion of a "kingdom of ends" as an idealization of association in terms of *societas*.

The ideal of *universitas*, by contrast, is that of "corporate" association. A corporation is a body of persons associated in pursuit of a definite common purpose. Typical *universitates* would be: a guild, a joint-stock company, a university. In such a form of association the correctness of actions is not, as it is for a *societas*, a matter of their being permissible in the light of a code of conduct. It is rather a matter of how they contribute to reaching the goal the association is instituted to pursue. In a *universitas*, decisions are at bottom "managerial" and the standards for good performance instrumental.

Taken as a model for the state, the form of association represented by *societas* leads us to an understanding of the state as what Oakeshott calls a civil association. Seen in this light, a state is first and foremost an association of persons united in virtue of their mutual recognition of the authority of a common body of law. This body of law regulates the conduct of the associates in the pursuit of their self-chosen satisfactions; it does not prescribe what satisfactions are to be chosen. The laws are indifferent to the particular goals of the associates, not merely impartial. On this view, the function or, as Oakeshott likes to say, the "office" of government is to provide for the enforcement of this body of law and to constitute a forum in which the terms of association codified by the law (never completely or perfectly) can be further specified or amended.

As a political ideal, the *societas* conception of the state as a civil association is founded on respect for the value of the individual. And individuals are to be understood in terms of autonomy. An individual is an agent capable of shaping his own life, setting his own goals, and thus requiring the freedom to do so. Civil associates, then, necessarily recognize each other as self-directed agents and are, consequently, united in the equality of mutual respect.

If the state is seen as a *universitas*, a quite different conception of government emerges. Far from being the custodian of a code of *civility* that provides a framework for its subjects' pursuit of their self-chosen goals and satisfactions, the government becomes the active promoter of a definite, common, substantive purpose—economic development, mutual prosperity, enlightenment, or whatever. (This outlook comes very naturally to those who think of themselves as "practical.")

There are various substantive goals that a state, thus understood, might be thought to aim at. But the three main types are prefigured in the analogies for the relation of ruler to ruled that animate Plato's *Republic*. The economic/development goal is implicit in the analogy of shepherd to sheep or captain to crew; the educational in that of teacher to pupil; and the therapeutic, Professor Lasch's particular *bête noire*, in that of doctor to patient.

All, at bottom, are variants on a single master analogy, that of craftsman to material, and all, accordingly, lead in the end to a denial of the moral equality inherent in the idea of civil association. For what matters to the craftsman is the result. He imposes form by any technically efficient means on a body of more or less recalcitrant matter in virtue of knowledge that he alone is required to possess. The clay need not envision a pattern in order to be transformed into a pot. Only the craftsman need do that. Nor need the patient understand why the medicine is good for him for it to work its cure; indeed, he may even prefer not to take it.

This asymmetry with respect to knowledge, carried over into the political realm, becomes a moral asymmetry. Only the ruler need be recognizable as a true agent. This is the inevitable consequence of turning a political community into a teleocracy, an association directed toward the promotion of a common purpose, by reference to which governmental actions acquire an objective correctness, independently of any willingness on the part of the governed to acknowledge them, according to how efficiently they promote that purpose.

We may not see this if we fail to grasp the point of the distinction between *societas* and *universitas*. The distinction has to do with the kind of association the state is supposed to be, hence with the kind of ordering function government is called upon to fulfill. In Oakeshott's terminology, it has to do with the "office" of government and not, for example, with its "constitution"—i.e., the terms in which it legitimizes its authority to govern. Thus inroads on civil association and consequent changes in the relation of associates to the government and to one another are not made less significant by the government's having a democratic constitution, though many who incline to a conception of the state in terms of *universitas* often seem to suppose they are. Thus in reply to the charge that the organization of government for the promotion of economic development and public welfare threatens to turn citizens into pensioners of the state, it is often said that the whole undertaking would remain "democratic" as if the state ceases to be paternalistic if one votes occasionally for those who exercise its paternal (Oakeshott likes to say "lordly") authority.

There is, then, something deeply moral in the ideal of the state as a civil association. In my view, the strength and value of the Liberal political order lies in the fact that it constitutes a no doubt imperfect and qualified but nevertheless recognizable embodiment of this ideal, by no means the only possible embodiment but the only one we have, indeed the only extant form of political life that accords the ideal of civil association any real respect or even allows for its uninhibited articulation and defense. It is therefore not to be lightly cast aside, least of all in the name of some shadowy, romantic, and inchoate "radical" alternative.

But what of liberal progressivism? I think there are two ways to look at this political tendency within the Liberal order. One way is to see it as heir to the eighteenth century tradition of "enlightened" government, technically efficient interventionist government conducted in the presumed interest of the governed. Viewed this way, liberal progressivism represents an understanding of the state in terms of *universitas*, with the result that liberal progressivism appears to exist in tension with Liberalism. But liberal progressivism can also be seen as importantly qualified by a commitment to the ideal of civil association—as recognizing its value but recognizing also that it will not, in modern times, be realizable if no regard is paid to the economic and social conditions of life.

In this connection, it is important to see that there is no necessary connection between an understanding of the state in terms of *societas* and a doctrinaire commitment to free market economic theories. As Oakeshott himself points out, advocates of the market may accept an entirely managerial view of the political order: the nation as development corporation for the efficient exploitation of natural and human resources. On this view, the office of government is restricted to maintaining the conditions under which the market can function with optimum efficiency and providing whatever necessary goods and services (national defense, for example) the market cannot be depended upon to produce reliably or at all. In this managerial conception, the market advocate may be joined by some liberal progressives and even some socialists (for example, of the Bellamy type), the only question at issue between them being the *technical* question of what degree and manner of government intervention in economic life maximizes output, employment, and so on. Or if there is a moral issue, it will be that of "distributive" justice: the question of how to allocate the benefits that it is supposedly the business of the nation to produce and the paternal state to dispense. But the fundamental idea of civil association is conduct regulated by law, not in the interest of some collective goal but to create a situation in which self-chosen goals may be pursued, alone or in cooperation with others. Business enterprise falls under the heading of "conduct" and so enjoys no special exemption from legal regulation.

To expand on this, it is surely true that where there is civil association there must be private property. Expressing and developing one's individuality in a self-chosen and self-directed life is impossible when all resources are at the command of the political authorities and subject to permanent and intrusive constraints imposed by some overriding public purpose. More than this, a Liberal will be wary of intervention in any aspect of life, of any contraction of the realm of individual choice. But none of this precludes his recognizing that vast and unregulated concentrations of economic wealth and power, either in view of the way their holders behave or perhaps in virtue of their very existence, can threaten the social conditions that sustain the tradition of civility that alone makes civil association possible. If he does come to perceive such a danger, he will want to take corrective action, though judiciously and in as limited a fashion as may be.

Similarly, just as Liberalism does not preclude making business enterprise (as everything else) subject to law, it does not rule out aid to the indigent. Along with recurrent wars, the problem of the poor, complicated and in some ways exacerbated by the emergence of industrial mass societies, has been a constant threat to the ideal of civil association. Nothing, however, prevents an upholder of civil association from realizing that the tradition of civility he so prizes is unlikely to flourish in the face of widespread and chronic poverty and insecurity, or from therefore advocating judicious measures directed toward their relief. He may even recognize that under modern conditions poverty is apt to become more relative than absolute and so be willing to countenance welfare provisions considerably more extensive than would be required simply to protect citizens from destitution.

Again, though, he will want to intervene judiciously to correct such problems. His reaction is essentially defensive and compassionate, not the first step toward some utopian goal. For those committed to some teleocratic view of the state, this kind of reformism (characteristic of what I have been calling liberal progressivism) will never go "far enough." It will seem to be condemned to improvization. But this is because, not being goal-directed, it is a continuing rather than a completable undertaking, the never-to-be finished task of adapting a state approximating the ideal of civil association to conditions that will continue to change in unforeseen ways.

Along these lines, the kind of legislation associated with liberal progressivism can be contingently defended. Lasch, we may recall, sees theoretical incoherence here. He sees "Liberalism" as pulled in contrary directions by "the claim that property-holders are entitled to enjoy the fruits of their enterprise with a minimum of interference from the state" and "the claim that the state has an obligation to provide less fortunate members of society . . . with 'liberty and opportunity, income and wealth, . . . the bases of self-respect.'"[4] Clearly, there is all the difference in the world between the way the state provides "liberty" and the way it might provide "income," and if there is any conflict in Liberalism it must arise from its recognizing an obligation to provide the latter rather than the former. But as I see it there is no need to think of Liberalism as recognizing any such unconditional obligation. All a Liberal need have is a willingness to countenance programs with such an effect in certain circumstances, and only then so as to defend his more fundamental values (and also perhaps to ensure that the freedom to shape one's own life is not for some people entirely notional).

There are, however, deeper ways in which Lasch misunderstands the Liberal political order.

Let us begin with his claim that the Liberal order "lacks a public philosophy." In one sense this must be true. If the Liberal order is a form of civil association, and if to have a "public philosophy" is to recognize a common substantive purpose for the state and its citizens to promote, then obviously a Liberal polity must lack a public philosophy. But that this is a deficiency remains to be shown. Even in point of mere stability and internal peace, Liberal states enjoy clear advantages over countries founded on "public philosophies," at least if the comparative mildness of the criminal law, the absence of a secret police, etc. are anything to go by. There is, however, another way of having a public philosophy: namely, subscribing in common with one's fellow citizens to a code of conduct or civility, formally though never exhaustively articulated in a body of law whose authority the citizens recognize, and which, while it does not specify what goals, individual or collective, are to be pursued, imposes conditions to be observed in the pursuit of any goals. Liberal states with their "formal" freedoms and their emphasis on the rule of law depend on just such a public philosophy. And, in an important sense, this kind of public philosophy must be more genuinely public than is necessary in a teleocratic state. A civil association depends on the citizens' recognizing themselves as united by their mutual recognition of the authority of a common body of law and other prescriptions relating to conduct. By contrast, the "citizen" of a teleocratic state need not necessarily recognize the "legitimacy" of or even so much as understand the managerial directives of the enlightened ruler. For to such a ruler, those at his command are less subjects to be ruled than materials to be organized, even if in their own best interests. Indeed, there is an inherent tendency in the teleocratic state to reduce political discourse to propaganda. Speech, like any other action, is subject only to instrumental assessment.

It seems to me, then, that in so far as Lasch produces an impression of Liberalism's incoherence, he does so by assimilating it to an inappropriate model of association. He assumes from the outset an understanding of the state in terms of *universitas*: hence his references to "the common needs of the community" and the implied desirability of articulating "a theory of the good society." But the articulation of such theories is no business of the Liberal state, in so far as it embodies the ideal of civil association. In effect, Lasch takes the Liberal state to be a corporate enterprise association, organized in pursuit of a common goal or goals, and then complains that, because of its regard for the individual, it has no way of determining what the goals should be or allocating the costs incurred by and benefits derived from their pursuit. This is incoherent, but it is also not Liberalism.

That this is how Lasch understands the Liberal order is evident, I think, from his tracing Liberalism's difficulties to "the incompatible claims that can be founded on an appeal to the interests of the individual (the only basis of social policy that liberalism acknowledges)."[5] Here the Liberal state is identified with an enterprise association for the satisfaction of interests, such that those who fail to derive sufficient benefits from the undertaking (the disappointed or even swindled stock holders, as it were) will feel and perhaps even be entitled to complain.

There is also evidence here of a deep misrepresentation of the philosophical basis of the Liberal order. This has to do with the reference to the *interests* of the individual. Lasch is not very explicit about this, but the whole tone of his discussion suggests to me that he accepts the view that the Liberal order is founded on a doctrine of "possessive individualism," itself deriving from a conception of human beings as at bottom (egoistically) motivated by appetites. From this standpoint, the Liberal state emerges as a framework for guaranteeing individuals the opportunity to satisfy whatever appetites they can, thus as devoted primarily to the protection of property.

Here, as elsewhere, *les extrêmes se touchent*, for this identification of the basis of the Liberal order is accepted by many who by no means share Lasch's attitude toward Liberalism. Spokesmen for "conservative" positions sometimes tell us that modern philosophy, or at least that part of it that leads to Liberalism, having rejected all transcendental sources of value, is able to recognize nothing beyond the satisfaction of bodily appetites as a basis for political association. But no defender of the Liberal order, certainly no one who values it as a form of civil association, need accept such an account of its basis. The basis of civil association is the individual understood as an agent capable of intelligent choice. Such an agent is understood as *für sich* and not merely *an sich*—i.e., not as the focus of a fixed "nature" but as inventing and disclosing himself in the life adventure in which (alone or with others) he is engaged, as constituted not by what he "is" but by what he understands himself to be, as fully characterized not solely by biological drives but by the self-descriptions he is willing to acknowledge. There is no necessary connection between the Liberal order and a philosophical anthropology so often denounced as vulgar and demeaning.

In conclusion, let me say a couple of things about Lasch's critique of the culture of Liberalism. We must, I think, concede that Lasch has a point. However, I do not think that the tendency to take on condescending attitudes he detects in some liberal progressives need be understood simply as a self-deceptive stratagem for disguising political failures. Rather, such a tendency can be traced to a regrettable proclivity on the part of liberal progressives for flirting with teleocratic conceptions of government; in this instance, an itch to make the state the vehicle for compulsory enlightenment.

As we have seen, the idea of civil association depends on a conception of human individuals as intelligent agents capable of participation in a moral practice. Furthermore, participation in such a practice involves the recognition of intelligent agency in both oneself and one's fellow practitioners, hence mutual respect. But a state as teleocracy requires no such mutual recognition. What matters is whether or not the body politic is achieving the goal it is constituted to pursue. Consequently there is always room for a moral asymmetry between the enlightened rulers and the human material they shape. But this suggests that liberal progressivism ought to reaffirm its links with Liberalism, hence with the idea of civil association, not seek to transcend it. This seems to me to be particularly evident with respect to the values (for example, values connected with family and neighborhood) that Professor Lasch would like to rescue. These "values" are not to be appropriated by some goal-directed politics for they are less values in an abstract sense than particular loyalties and attachments. They are best defended by defending a polity that recognizes the importance of life outside the realm of politics.

These remarks in defense of the Liberal order and the liberal tendency within it can properly be called "conservative," though perhaps not in the most currently popular sense of that term. What passes for conservatism in America today, however, is a curious mixture of classical economic theory and religious fundamentalism. Neither element in this mixture can be depended on as a support of the Liberal order. However, much of the attitude to the Liberal order I have tried to convey can be found in what is sometimes called "neo-conservative" political writing. The attitude is one of respect for the political values of Liberalism and for the achievements of Liberal culture. For one with this attitude, the Liberal order is something to be sustained, defended, and where possible improved, not lightly cast aside. In so far as liberal progressivism has contributed to sustaining the Liberal order, the same can be said for it too.

Notes

1. Christopher Lasch, "Liberalism in Retreat," chapter 7, this volume. All discussion of Lasch refers to this essay.

2. Ibid., p. 105.

3. Michael Oakeshott, *On Human Conduct* (Oxford: Clarendon Press, 1975). See especially ch. 3, "On the Character of a Modern European State."

4. Lasch, "Liberalism in Retreat," p. 105.

5. Ibid.

9

A "Non-Lockean" Locke and the Character of Liberalism

NATHAN TARCOV

Louis Hartz characterized the liberal tradition in America as Lockean.[1] That characterization of the American founding and of the political life that followed it, powerful and illuminating as it is, is not exhaustive or precise. Many elements in the American founding and American political life, of course, are not specifically Lockean.[2] But the legitimate search for non-Lockean elements must be based on a genuine picture of our Lockean heritage and not on a caricature. One should not proceed as if anything other than the most self-interested, atomistic, hedonistic, materialistic individualism required a non-Lockean label.

Misunderstanding of Lockean liberalism helps to stimulate not only the historical search for non-Lockean elements in the American tradition but also the political dissatisfaction with liberalism. Not everyone can be satisfied by an understanding of man as an asocial individual dedicated solely to the unlimited accumulation of property and by an understanding of society as an aggregate of such individuals and an arena for the pursuit and compromise of their interests. Critics from the right reject liberalism to find a place for churches, families, and moral virtue. Critics from the left reject it to find a place for community and the common good. Liberalism cannot be all things to all men, but it does not have to refuse all satisfaction to those who reject its "Lockean" form. Indeed, a reexamination of John Locke's own liberal political theory suggests the possibility of a broader, deeper, and loftier liberalism.

An earlier version of this essay was presented at the Hampden-Sydney College Symposium on the Origin and Character of Modern Republicanism, April 8–9, 1981. I have benefited from the criticisms and suggestions of Ruth Grant and Thomas Pangle and of Douglas MacLean and Claudia Mills of the Center for Philosophy and Public Policy at the University of Maryland.

This essay seeks to correct several central misunderstandings of Locke that contribute to the false picture of Lockean liberalism described above. Locke's political teaching is *not* one of self-interest but one of *rights*. Argument from interest rather than rights represents a degradation of Lockean politics and of the political theory of our nation's founding. Lockean politics include a conception of the common good and a conception of civil society as more than an aggregate of atomistic individuals. His understanding of human nature exhibits a profound appreciation of human sociality, and families and churches play crucial roles in Lockean civil society. Locke teaches not a narrowly calculating selfishness but a set of decent moral virtues. Nor is his fundamental concern with property the justification of money-grubbing.

It can be argued that Lockean liberalism's fundamental concern for individual liberty ultimately undermines the "non-Lockean" elements I stress. Showing the presence of such elements in Locke's texts cannot by itself demonstrate that liberalism must rise above self-interest and crass materialism and make a place for the common good and human sociality, but recovery of the surface of Locke's texts can help open our minds to that possibility.

Rights and Interests

To understand Locke's liberal political theory in the *Second Treatise* as one of self-interest or even of interest generally is to misunderstand fundamentally what kind of work Locke thought he was writing. In "Some Thoughts Concerning Reading and Study for a Gentleman," Locke divides politics into "two parts very different the one from the other, the one containing the original of societies and the rise and extent of political power, the other, the art of governing men in society."[3] He describes that first part of politics (in *Some Thoughts Concerning Education*) as instruction in "the natural Rights of Men, and the Original and Foundations of Society, and the Duties resulting from thence."[4] Thus by Locke's own account, the political teaching of the *Second Treatise* (titled *An Essay Concerning the True Original, Extent, and End of Civil Government*) is not fundamentally a prudential teaching about interests but a moral or legal (though pertaining to natural law) teaching about rights and duties. Locke's political theory is deontological rather than utilitarian.

The most basic argument of Locke's liberal political theory is about *rights*. The fundamental hypothesis of the *Two Treatises* is the natural freedom of men, that is, their *right* to be free until they consent to political subjection.[5] That consent is rationally given only to protect their lives, liberty, and property,[6] which in turn Locke presents not as interests but as rights. Life is the "Right of Self-preservation";

liberty is the "Right of my Freedom"; property is the "Right of Property."[7]

The importance Locke gives to the right to self-preservation may have led some to confuse his theory with later doctrines of self-interest, for he seems to derive rights to liberty and property from the fundamental right to self-preservation. Freedom is "the Fence to" preservation, "necessary to, and closely joyned with a Man's preservation."[8] According to Locke, "I have reason to conclude, that he who would get me into his Power without my consent, would . . . destroy me too when he had a fancy to" if only because "I have no reason to suppose that he, who would *take away my Liberty*, would not when he had me in his Power, take away every thing else."[9] That right to defend oneself against the worst possible case is the basis of the liberal reasoning about limiting power in the name of liberty, familiar from every parade of horribles used to argue against power because of the danger of its extension or abuse. Man's right to property is derived in the first place directly from his right to preservation as a right to things "necessary or useful to his Being" or for "the Subsistence and Comfort of his Life."[10] Property in other things is derived as well from one's "Property in his own Person," that is, body, by way of the *"Labour* of his Body," which is the "unquestionable Property of the Labourer."[11]

The right to self-preservation is not the same as self-interest, however. It is true that Locke undergirds this right with a desire: "the first and strongest desire God planted in Men . . . being that of Self-preservation."[12] But he does not reduce the right to that desire. Rights for Locke are not, like rights for Hobbes, free of correlative duties for others to respect them. Even Hobbes means by the right to self-preservation not merely the factual claim that all men have a natural desire for self-preservation, but the additional moral claim that no one can be blamed for following that desire. The moral component in Locke's right is so strong that he often presents self-preservation not merely as a right but as a law or a duty. He argues that men have no right, liberty, or power to give up their own lives or to give up the necessary means, such as liberty, to their preservation.[13]

Locke's attributions of rights differ from assertions of interest in that they include correlative duties of others to respect them. The rights to life, liberty, and property are accompanied by duties to respect the lives, liberty, and property of others.[14] A man's duty toward others comes into operation "when his own Preservation comes not in competition" and is subject to the qualification "as much as he can."[15] But it is not therefore negligible. The crucial task of Locke's liberal politics is to construct conditions where the duties of self-preservation and the duties to preserve others are least in competition—"well order'd" governments in contrast to the state of nature or absolute monarchies.[16]

The misunderstanding of Locke's teaching of rights and duties as a teaching of self-interest is furthered by his calling the rights of life, liberty, and property all by the one word "property," as he explicitly notes that he does.[17] Locke's choice of the single term "property," however, is far from making the triad more a matter of interest and less a matter of rights. We have already seen that property in the narrow sense (which Locke sometimes calls "estate" to make the distinction clear) is itself a matter of right. It is indeed not only a right, but a "private right," one that explicitly excludes the rights of others.[18] Property is defined as that which cannot be rightfully taken from one without one's own consent.[19] One's right to property implies a corollary restriction on the right of others, that is, a duty for them to respect one's right. In this way property in the narrow sense is the proper model for all rights.[20]

Liberalism can still contain a theory of interest while being fundamentally a theory of rights. The notion of interest plays an important role in the *Two Treatises*, but one still subordinate to the central argument about rights and duties. Most of Locke's statements about interest are what we might call pathological rather than prescriptive. They explain various obstacles in the way of a more rational order of government and limitations on how government may be legitimated: Locke admits ruefully that "a great part" of the positive laws of countries do not follow reason or the law of nature, but are "the Phansies and intricate Contrivances of Men, following contrary and hidden interests put into Words";[21] he concedes that "the variety of Opinions, and contrariety of Interests, which unavoidably happen in all Collections of Men" preclude the foundation of society on unanimous consent.[22]

The most important and recurrent pathological use Locke makes of the notion of interest is in warning against the abuse of political power by rulers who serve their own interests at the expense of their subjects'. He writes that

> where the *legislative* is in one lasting Assembly always in being, or in one Man, as in Absolute Monarchies, there is danger still, that they will think themselves to have a distinct interest, from the rest of the Community.[23]

In similar terms he warns that

> it may be too great a temptation to humane frailty apt to grasp at Power, for the same Persons who have the Power of making Laws, to have also in their hands the power to execute them, whereby they may exempt themselves from Obedience to the Laws they make, and suit the Law, both in its making and execution, to their own private

advantage, and thereby come to have a distinct interest from the rest of the Community.[24]

The doctrine that princes have a "distinct and separate Interest from the good of the Community" is, on Locke's view, "the Root and Source, from which spring almost all those Evils, and Disorders, which happen in Kingly Governments."[25]

Locke describes well-ordered politics not as a process involving distinct and separate political interests, but as the protection of private rights and the exercise of power for the common good. Cases of distinct and separate political interests are cases of poorly ordered conditions that give rise to evils and disorders. Locke's liberal politics has in common with theories of interest the view that men are sufficiently self-interested, or so love power and wealth, that a condition that makes it in their interest to be unjust will likely find them unjust. But the *desideratum* for his liberal politics is construction of a condition where such interests are not encouraged. He resolves this question by an appeal not to self-interest, but to right or the public interest.

Community and the Common Good

The public interest or common good therefore plays a crucial role in Locke's political theory, as it must in any liberal political theory that succeeds in regulating self-interest. Indeed, the most common use Locke makes of the notion of interest is precisely that of the public interest or interest of the whole community; the *Second Treatise* is full of invocations of the public or common good.[26] The closest Locke comes to defining the public good is, however, in the *First Treatise*, where he writes of the public good as "the good of every particular Member of that Society, as far as by common Rules, it can be provided for."[27] The common good Locke invokes is very individualist, very close to the notion of the protection of the lives, liberties, and properties of all the individual members "as far as possible." But it is not simply an additive sum of prepolitical private rights. It includes these only insofar as they can be protected by general laws or other appropriate public actions. And it includes as well the preservation of society itself as a body and of its laws and institutions.

Locke does not understand civil society as simply an aggregate of atomistic individuals, unlike those liberals who reject notions of unity or community or those lovers of unity and community who reject liberal civil society. Civil society has a common good that justifies thinking of it as a whole to which individuals understood as parts may have to be sacrificed.[28] For Locke, government exists "for the benefit of the Governed . . . as they make a part of that Politick

Body, each of whose parts and Members are taken care of, and directed in its peculiar Functions for the good of the whole, by the Laws of the Society."[29]

Locke emphasizes the intended unity and permanence of civil society. When men "*make one Community* or Government, they are thereby presently incorporated, and make *one Body Politick* . . . one Body, with a Power to Act as one Body . . . one Body, *one Community* . . . one Body Politick under one Government . . . *one Society.*"[30] This unity depends on the fact that

> in a Constituted Commonwealth, standing upon its own Basis, and acting according to its own Nature, that is, acting for the preservation of the Community, there can be but *one Supream Power*, which is *the Legislative.*[31]

Locke explains that it is

> in their *Legislative*, that the Members of a Commonwealth are united, and combined together into one coherent living Body. This *is the Soul that gives Form, Life, and Unity* to the Commonwealth: From hence the several Members have their mutual Influence, Sympathy, and Connexion.[32]

The permanence of civil society is intended because we cannot think "that Rational Creatures should desire and constitute Societies only to be dissolved."[33] As a corollary, an individual who has once given explicit consent to be a member of any commonwealth "is perpetually and indispensably obliged to be and remain unalterably a Subject to it" unless it is dissolved contrary to its intention through some "Calamity" or he is excommunicated from it.[34] This intended unity and permanence of civil society seems to underlie the strict prohibition against the rulers' merging the commonwealth into another.[35]

Locke's liberalism departs from the atomistic model also in the important roles he gives to families and churches. We are accustomed to think of liberal individualism as dissolving the authority and even the existence of the family and the church. But the protection of individual liberty from coercive authority may itself require strong families and churches. One might argue that the fundamental separation of powers in the *Two Treatises* is between education, which Locke gives to the family but not to government, and the power of life and death, which he gives to government but not to the family.[36] Locke not only defends politics from the authoritarian implications of the model of the patriarchal family, but also protects the family from authoritarian government. He presents himself as the defender of the family against Filmer, who by identifying paternal with political power seemed to abolish the family, and proclaims that "the most Absolute Power of Princes cannot absolve us" from our duty to our parents. Parental power "contains nothing of the Magistrates Power in it, nor is subjected to it."[37] Similarly, when Locke, in *A Letter Concerning Toleration*, forbids civil government from teaching religion to children, he grants that function not to self-educating, atomistic individuals but to parents. The education he recommends in *Some Thoughts Concerning Education* is emphatically a domestic education performed by and within the family. The argument for toleration denies concern for salvation to civil government, but assumes that it will typically be pursued by men in voluntary groups called churches, not simply as individuals.

The study of Locke also indicates that one does not have to go outside of liberalism to find a place for human sociality, indeed, that liberalism is stronger when it is based on an understanding of human nature like Locke's that includes a profound appreciation not only of human individuality but also of human sociality. This awareness of human sociality is found most clearly and richly in *Some Thoughts Concerning Education*. The whole education Locke proposes rests on the recognition that *"Esteem* and *Disgrace* are, of all others, the most powerful Incentives to the Mind, when once it is brought to relish them. If you can once get into Children a Love of Credit, and an Apprehension of Shame and Disgrace," Locke continues, "you have put into them the true Principle, which will constantly work, and incline them to the right."[38] Lockean psychology is hedonistic, but the most powerful pleasures and pains are not the purely private ones of the body or even of the accumulation or loss of property, but the social ones of esteem and disgrace.

According to a liberal political theory like Locke's, government is concerned not with the cultivation of moral virtues but with the protection of rights. Education is a private rather than a public power. The end of civil society, as is made clear in *A Letter Concerning Toleration*, is the protection of the life, liberty, and property of its members, the rights pertaining to the body, and not the improvement or salvation of the soul. But that fundamental limitation of liberal political theory does not mean that it is indifferent to education, especially to moral education and the virtues it teaches. Rights imply duties; liberalism can secure individual liberty best when individuals are educated to the moral virtues that lead them to respect each other's rights.

In the *Thoughts*, where Locke addresses not rulers or subjects as such but parents, he is concerned above all with moral education and places *"Vertue* as the first and most necessary of those Endowments, that belong to a Man or a Gentleman; as absolutely requisite to make him valued and beloved by others, acceptable or tolerable to himself."[39] He also says there, " 'Tis Vertue then, direct Vertue, which is the hard and valuable part to be aimed at in Education. . . . All other Considerations and Accomplishments should give way and be postpon'd to this."[40] Although education is not the business of politics, Locke recognizes in the Epistle Dedicatory that "the Welfare and Prosperity of the Nation so much depends on it, that I would have every one lay it seriously to Heart" and explains that he himself published the *Thoughts* as part of his effort to fulfill "every Man's indispensible Duty, to do all the Service he can to his Country."

Instead of a narrowly calculating selfishness, Locke teaches a set of moral virtues that make men able to respect themselves and be useful to one another both in private and in public life. These virtues include the liberal virtues of justice, civility, liberality, and humanity as well as the familiar "bourgeois" virtues of self-denial, industriousness, and thrift. They are taught on the basis of not only the egoistic sensibility to pleasure, pain, fear, and concern for self-preservation, but also the more positive social concerns for esteem and liberty, as well as morally ambiguous but equally social ambition and emulation.

Although these virtues are not taught in a directly political context, they directly address the problems of Locke's liberal politics. Locke does not teach these virtues, even justice, on the basis of patriotism or directly teach the love of country itself, as does Plato in the *Republic* or Rousseau in *The Government of Poland*. He apparently expects the love of country to which he appeals in the Epistle Dedicatory of the *Thoughts* to grow out of men's private attachments. But the virtues he teaches serve the same goals as his liberal politics: securing the rights to preservation of oneself and others and avoiding the injustice and contention that disturb human life.

The *Two Treatises* present "the Natural Vanity and Ambition of Men," the passion or imagination that substitutes for reason, and the fancy or covetousness that desires the benefits of others' labor, as the chief psychological roots of the political threats to the rights of life, liberty, and property. These are precisely the tendencies that the Lockean moral virtues are intended to counter. Self-preservation rests solidly on the "first and strongest desire God planted in Men," but the natural duty to preserve others, at least apart from one's own children, does not seem to have any similar basis in human nature.[41] The moral education Locke provides in the *Thoughts* is his complex account of how to build on a solid basis in human nature a concern for the rights of others.

This account of Locke's liberal theory may seem contrary to his reputation as a defender of capitalism. But Locke does not teach crass materialism or justify "capitalism" as the unlimited accumulation of property for its own sake. The primary purposes of his doctrine of property are rather to deny that property "gives a Man Power over the Life of another"[42] and to assert a natural as opposed to a divine title to property.[43] He affirms that governments are to "regulate" property[44] and derives the right to property from the right to life, to which it is subordinate.[45] Locke's liberalism is not identified with a narrowly conceived capitalism that puts property above life and liberty.

Far from identifying rationality with unlimited accumulation, Locke regards it as closely connected to human sociality and love of liberty. He writes in the *Thoughts* that "We would be thought Rational Creatures, and have our Freedom."[46] Human pride expresses itself above all as a desire to be esteemed by others as free and rational.

Both contemporary political dissatisfaction with liberalism and the historical search for non-Lockean elements in the American tradition rest in part on the dominant interpretations of the moral vision of Lockean liberalism, which attribute to Locke a mean-spirited selfish materialism. Finding nothing decent or inspiring in the interpretations of Locke, students of our political culture have gone off seeking after "non-Lockean" elements in our heritage. We may begin instead with the "non-Lockean" elements in Locke.

It was not unLockean when Americans declared their independence in the name not of interests but of the inalienable rights which governments are instituted to secure. If life, liberty, and the pursuit of happiness were understood merely as interests, the signers would not have pledged their lives, fortunes, and sacred honor to defend them. It was not unLockean when Publius made the most famous American argument about interests in *Federalist* 10 in the context of securing justice or private rights and the public good.[47] It *was* unLockean when John Taylor of Caroline suppressed Jefferson's recognition of the natural rights of all men in order to argue for slavery on the level of interest.[48] It was not unLockean when Henry Clay argued that Americans had to support liberty around the world, in South America, Liberia, and Greece, because liberty is not merely an interest but a right shared by all mankind. It was not unLockean when Lincoln taught Americans to side with liberty as a universal right rather than with self-interest. Arguments from a ground higher than interest and a sense of community do not require a non-Lockean source. They can be arguments from the natural rights and common good of Lockean liberalism.

One should not ask how a supposedly "Lockean" America can contain such "non-Lockean" elements as concern for the public good, sociality, moral virtue, and government regulation. One should ask instead how America got from the loftier and broader concerns of a Lockean founding to a later narrowly atomistic and materialistic self-interest.

Notes

1. Louis Hartz, *The Liberal Tradition in America* (New York: Harcourt, Brace, and World, 1955).

2. Garry Wills has tried to substitute the Scottish enlightenment thinkers for Locke as the inspiration for Jefferson's Declaration of Independence. Garry Wills, *Inventing America: Jefferson's Declaration of Independence* (New York: Vintage Books, 1979). Ronald Hamowy's critique of Wills shows that Locke cannot be so easily replaced. See "Jefferson and the Scottish Enlightenment: A Critique of Garry Wills's *Inventing America*," *William and Mary Quarterly* ser. 3, vol. 36 (October 1979): 503–23.

3. John Locke, "Some Thoughts Concerning Reading and Study for a Gentleman," in *The Educational Writings of John Locke*, edited by James L. Axthell (Cambridge: Cambridge University Press, 1968), p. 400.

4. John Locke, *Some Thoughts Concerning Education*, #186.

5. John Locke, *First Treatise*, 2, 3, 4, 13, 67; *Second Treatise*, 4, 87. Hereafter, 1T, 2T.

6. 2T, 88, 123–24, 127, 134, 136–38, 140, 171.

7. 2T, 11, 17, 45, 50.

8. 2T, 17, 23.

9. 2T, 17–18.

10. 2T, 25; 1T, 86, 92.

11. 2T, 27.

12. 1T, 86, 88.

13. 2T, 6, 23, 135, 149, 168, 172.

14. E.g., 2T, 6–7, 11.

15. 2T, 6.

16. 2T, 143; cf. 94, 111, 159.

17. 2T, 87, 173.

18. 2T, 27, 28, 34.

19. 2T, 32, 138–40, 193.

20. Locke presents other rights in the *Second Treatise* besides the fundamental and famous triad of life, liberty, and property. The most important is probably "the Right of War" (2T, 16, 18, 19), which is identical to the right of resistance against force without right, the defense of which is the culmination of the book (2T, 192, 207–8, 220, 232). Locke also discusses the rights and duties of parents and children, the right to inherit one's father's goods (2T, 190), and even the right to a legislature chosen by majority consent (2T, 176). Nor does he neglect to mention the "Rights of Government" (2T, 111).

21. 2T, 12. Cf. 2T, 157–58, where Locke holds "private interest" responsible for "keeping up Customs and Priviledges, when the reasons of them are ceased" and finds a remedy for it in an executive who "sincerely follows" the maxim "*Salus Populi Suprema Lex*" and acts "not by old custom, but true reason."

22. 2T, 98.

23. 2T, 138.

24. 2T, 143. See also 111.

25. 2T, 163, 164.

26. 2T, 3, 89, 110, 130–31, 135, 137, 142–43, 156, 158–60, 162–67, 200, 215, 222, 239.

27. 1T, 92.

28. Civil society may be thought of as a whole because the duty to preserve others does not entail absolute duties to individuals. The qualification that a man in the state of nature ought to preserve others "as much as he can" includes the recognition that the preservation of as much of mankind as possible may require the destruction of some (2T, 6; cf. 8, 11, 16, 18). This qualification applies also to civil society itself, whose power is "for the preservation of the property of all the Members of that Society, as far as is possible" or "as far as will consist with the publick good" or "as much as may be" (2T, 88, 134, 159). Not only is the duty of civil society directed toward its own members rather than toward all mankind, but it may require laws which "tend to the preservation of the whole, but cutting off those Parts, and those only, which are so corrupt, that they threaten the sound and healthy" (2T, 171).

Although "even the guilty are to be spared, where it can prove no prejudice to the innocent" (2T, 159), "the safety of the Innocent is to be preferred" (2T, 16). This may include the destruction not only of ordinary criminals, but of foreign aggressors and tyrants (2T, 172, 182, 230). It may even require the sacrifice of the innocent in one's own army or in other circumstances of emergency (2T, 139, 159). A majority may refrain from exercising the right of resistance and tolerate "examples of particular Injustice, or Oppression of here and there an unfortunate Man" (2T, 230; cf. 208).

29. 1T, 93.
30. 2T, 95–97.
31. 2T, 149; cf. 134, 150.
32. 2T, 212.
33. 2T, 98.
34. 2T, 121.
35. 2T, 217.
36. 1T, 52–54; 2T, 56, 58, 65, 68, 170–71, 173–74.
37. 1T, 64–66.
38. *Some Thoughts Concerning Education*, #56.
39. Ibid., #135.
40. Ibid., #70.
41. 1T, 10, 58, 88; 2T, 34, 107, 111, 199, 230.
42. 1T, 41–43, 73, 92–93, 97; 2T, 72–73.
43. 1T, 21–43, 85–92; 2T, 25, 39.
44. 2T, 3, 38, 45, 139.
45. 1T, 42–43, 86, 88; 2T, 25.
46. *Some Thoughts* #41; cf. ##76, 81, 98, 119, 148, 167.
47. Locke, too, seems to identify justice with the protection of men's rights. 2T, 219.
48. Compare John Taylor, *Arator*, Number 14, to Thomas Jefferson, *Notes on the State of Virginia*, query 18.

Index

Notes on Contributors

WALTER BERNS is a Resident Scholar at the American Enterprise Institute and a Professorial Lecturer at Georgetown University. He is the author of *For Capital Punishment; Freedom, Virtue, and the First Amendment;* and *Constitutional Cases in American Government.*

MARSHALL COHEN is Professor of Philosophy at the City University of New York and was a founding editor of *Philosophy & Public Affairs.* He is the coeditor of numerous books, including *The Rights and Wrongs of Abortion, War and Moral Responsibility,* and *Marx, Justice, and History.*

RONALD DWORKIN is Professor of Jurisprudence at Oxford University and Professor of Law at New York University. He is the author of the very influential recent book *Taking Rights Seriously.*

AMY GUTMANN is Associate Professor of Politics at Princeton University and is the author of *Liberal Equality.*

CHRISTOPHER LASCH is Professor of History at the University of Rochester. His many books include *The Culture of Narcissism* and *Haven in a Heartless World.*

MARK SAGOFF is Research Associate at the Center for Philosophy and Public Policy at the University of Maryland. He has published numerous articles on aesthetics and environmental law.

THEDA SKOCPOL is Associate Professor of Sociology and Political Science at the University of Chicago and author of *States and Revolutions.*

NATHAN TARCOV is Associate Professor of Political Science at the University of Chicago. From April 1981 to June 1982 he was a member of the Policy Planning Staff of the Department of State. He is the author of a forthcoming book on Locke.

MICHAEL WILLIAMS is Associate Professor of Philosophy at the University of Maryland. He is the author of *Groundless Belief.*